THROUGH
THE EYE
OF
A NEEDLE

Derek Farrow

THROUGH

THE EYE

OF

A NEEDLE

A short study of
a Christian approach
to money

London EPWORTH PRESS

© Methodist Ministers' Housing Society 1979
Royalties from the sale of this book are donated
to the Methodist Ministers' Housing Society.
First published 1979
by Epworth Press

7162 0322 7

Enquiries should be addressed to
The Methodist Publishing House
Wellington Road
Wimbledon
London SW19 8EU

Made and printed in Great Britain by
The Garden City Press Limited
Letchworth, Hertfordshire SG6 1JS

Preface

Although the Methodist Conference has honoured me with the appointment of General Secretary of the Division of Finance, a position I have held for a number of years, it is only fair to make clear that the views expressed in this book are entirely my own and do not necessarily represent the official policy of the Methodist Church.

This book would not have been written but for the patience and painstaking efforts of my Secretary, Mrs Olive Dew, and I also express my deep sense of indebtedness to colleagues, and particularly to my friend John Stacey, who has made numerous and helpful suggestions regarding the text of the book.

D.R.F.

Contents

For Irene

Introduction

'Take the waiting out of wanting' was a good advertising slogan for a particular credit card. It also vividly symbolised a new impatience for increased material wealth to which the modern man considered he had a right. It further suggested that anything that could speed gratification of the desire is good.

It is not surprising, after a precarious existence when man was toiling to achieve victory over hunger, cold, malnutrition and the serfdom of circumstance, that when comparative riches become a foreseeable goal many see no reason why they should not grasp what is going, and the sooner the better.

Now that industrial revolution has reached what is perhaps the summit of achievement in production, all seek to share in the spoils. Trades Unions have, particularly in the United Kingdom, found new strength, and exercise a powerful collective muscle to ensure that their members are not left behind.

The comparatively sudden explosion in the growth of riches for the ordinary individual, coupled with the advent of television, air travel, and other modern methods of communication, have however helped to make the world a smaller place. The average Christian in the western world has been presented with a new dimension to a problem that has tormented the conscience of a few of the rich, for centuries, namely, 'How much of my wealth is surplus to my needs, and how much am I bound by a sensitive religion to give away?' This is followed by a number of other awkward questions: 'How much attention ought one to pay to those who frequently and often colourfully present the needs of the Third World?' 'Economically how much

Through the eye of a needle

attention dare we pay to what they say?' 'Does our own hard work count for nothing on the scales of entitlement?' 'Are the humanitarian and cranky ecologists mere belly-achers likely to land us in vast unemployment if we take too much notice of them?', 'Are there any circumstances when a second car or a dishwasher is justified?' 'Should the possible exhaustion of the natural wealth in our age be of any consequence to us?' 'Many of these questions are being closely studied by church and inter-church groups and the discussion will continue for decades.

In this book, an attempt is made to consider some of these and other questions, not with the tongue of the preacher keen to argue a case and make a convert, nor with the formidable armoury of the defence counsel employed to maintain the status quo. Instead, it is hoped that what follows will appear as an honest attempt to enquire into what we do and why, and to present a balanced judgement relating to many of the problems which affect our use of money, interpreting this maligned means of exchange, and its related problems, from a Christian point of view—one finding ultimate significance in the life and teaching of Jesus.

To find some easy way to guiding principles is likely to be impossible. One literal application of the Gospel is, of course, to become a temporary saint and give all one has to feed the poor; but even with this simplistic approach one becomes thereafter a persistent nuisance to the community which is finally obliged to sustain even the voluntary poor. That is not to say it was not the answer to one man's problems at one point in history.

Whilst an appeal to scripture for guidance in complica-tions of modern economics is to say the least dangerous for some, even irrelevant: to others a re-interpretation of Christian teaching is always possible. Are we likely to find there any light regarding an ethical judgement of capital-ism or its alternative, communism? Our present economic system has, we are told, emerged from vigorous initiative leading to prudent savings meeting unsatisfied demand in the most efficient way possible.

Capitalism, however, has grown and become more powerful with many enterprises growing larger and larger to the point of increasing inefficiency. International companies often straddle continents but become, say some, an anonymous tyranny to a growingly inarticulate work force. The incoherence of frustration frequently leads to violence either of a physical kind, or, more likely, to the desire to take action through a strike which will attract attention. Has Christianity anything to offer those who seek to eradicate these evils? Does the teaching of Jesus favour, or point to even greater evils in, communism?

Confronted with the intractable issues surrounding economics, people are apt to blame 'money'—'Money is the root of all evil', to follow the favourite misquotation from St Paul. It is clear, however, that money has no life of its own: it is entirely dependent on the people who control it, and it reflects their attitudes to life. It is a measure of their efficiency, ruthlessness, compassion or lack of it, their optimism or pessimism, courage or cowardice; it is an indication of our priorities and points to the type of society we are working towards, either consciously or unconsciously.

To many, 'the City' appears as a very powerful entity, and occasionally international finance appears even more powerful. However, it is people and their policies that make the running and not money itself. Government can always ultimately control 'the City' and can change—and even ruin—business through its tax policies and other requirements. The policies of the City are the policies of major financiers, bankers and investors, but these are subservient to the policies and theories of the Government of the day which can manipulate and in the last resort destroy, the City. That is not to say the financiers would give up without a struggle, but in the last resort the Government would win, unless the people, reflected by the views of their M.P.s, thought the Government wrong.

Inflation, bull and bear markets and other phenomena associated with finance sometimes appear to have a life of their own and to be impervious to Government control. The conditions that engender and sustain such states are complex and often psychological in origin. A long slide in share prices (bear market) is often started by a series of events which induce pessimism. If the knocks to confidence have been severe enough and over a protracted enough period, then the ensuing pessimistic groove is not easy to escape from, especially if the overall economic state of the country is suspect; the slide continues, often to an exaggerated and unnecessary point. It might seem that such movements are unbridled and uncontrollable—often they are, but it is the people involved, together with their attitudes, which are responsible, and mass human behaviour always has been difficult to check and regulate.

Various views are taken on the ultimate cause of inflation, but there is no doubt that it is in some way caused by human action and does not spawn of its own volition. The inability of democratic governments to control their expenditure under pressure from the democracies they serve, is undoubtedly one of the most obvious causes, together with excessive wage demands. Christians, however, looking at the whole situation in non-economic terms, tend to describe the seething discontent and the Gadarene rush for more and more wages and goods, both those personally purchased as well as those publicly supplied, as a spiritual malaise.

Again, it would be naïve to assume that the simple application of a few rules of Christian behaviour would solve all our problems. What is possible, however, is that a clearer idea of how Christians should behave towards money would help to provide a stabilising influence in financial circles—especially if those ideas could be enunciated with a certain unity and clarity.

There are many roads leading to a Christian interpretation of economics. Jesus spoke frequently of 'the Kingdom'—that which was at hand—possibly in the sense of the 'near at hand' or in the sense of that which is eventually achievable to those who recognise God's rule. At no time did he annunciate a systematic formulation of behaviour to be expected within his Kingdom; still less did he lay down financial guidelines.

There is, however, sufficient guidance given to suggest a tentative approach to the formidable problem of all those with possessions emulating the camel in its attempt to pass through the eye of a needle. This struggle we should explore with a combination of curiosity and apprehension—the latter generated by the worrying knowledge that not only is the task impossible for man alone, but also that rarely does the Spirit of Christ favour 'the status quo', and rarely does encounter with God leave us entirely satisfied with our own personality and judgements.

It would be wrong to assume that this book seeks to give an authoritative answer to any of the problems associated with the use of money. It is not even a systematic study of the questions, but rather the reflections of one, initially tutored in the things of God, who has been required by his Church to deal with the things of mammon.

It cannot be said that the Church has been conspicuously successful in its efforts to apply the Gospel to the use of money. Even as early as the Acts of the Apostles there was hesitation and a feeling that money should be regarded as secondary to the 'real' work of the Kingdom. As it was not until the nineteenth century that the economic value of using capital was properly developed, it is not surprising that in the 1800 years that stretched from the time of Christ the Church followed the general misgivings relating to the lending and borrowing of money. Christians of the period would not have disputed Polonius's advice to Laertes:

> Neither a borrower, nor a lender be;
> for loan oft loses both itself and friend;
> and borrowing dulls the edge of husbandry.

Similarly, the opprobrium which was directed towards those who were engaged in the lending of money on a professional basis is seen very clearly in *The Merchant of Venice*. Shylock is portrayed as a grasping, uncompromising Jew who is completely devoid of all humanity and compassion and is despised by virtually everyone. Here was a graphic warning to all contemporaries not to get into the hands of such people.

As early as the Councils of Arles and Nicea in the fourth century the clergy were prohibited from lending money on interest. Condemnation of all loans with interest was made at the Council at Carthage in 348, and reinforced at the Third Lateran Council in 1179. To get round the prohibition, Jews were accepted as money-lenders even if they were somewhat hypocritically condemned for providing this service!

Some past attitudes to money

The bull of Pope Leo X later embodied in a decree of a General Council of the Roman Catholic Church (the 5th. Lateran Council 1512–17) defined usury as being 'when gain and fruit is sought, without labour, cost or risk, from the use of something which is not fruitful'. Lewis Watt, commenting in 1945 on usury in *Usury in Catholic Theology*, said: 'No Catholic theologian or economist would deny that usury is a form of injustice, and therefore evil.' Certainly before the Reformation the taking of any interest for the use of money was regarded as evil. In later years the definition of usury appears to have changed somewhat and is used particularly for the charging of interest at a higher than reasonable amount. Medieval theologians believed that it was unjust to attach to the sale of a fungible * thing a charge for the right to use it, over and above the just price of the thing itself. As money was thought of as a fungible thing, the just price of a sum of money was exactly the same sum, and therefore to take more money than that sum as a charge for the right to use it would have been unnecessary and unjust since the right to use it was necessarily transferred along with ownership. To attempt to use it by surrendering it, yet not parting with the ownership of it, was regarded as self-contradictory.

It was widely considered that money in itself was not productive. This of course would be categorically denied by modern economists. Money was widely regarded as sterile because it was not in itself fruitful and theologians dismissed any argument which maintained that it could represent something that was fruitful or be equivalently fruitful. All this tended to suggest that money was an entity in its own right, rather than as a token of something else—stored wealth or a coupon to exchange for some other kind of wealth. Too much emphasis in those days was placed upon money in the terms of the actual gold or silver

---

* 'Fungible' described something which was the subject of an obligation when something else of the same or another class could have been delivered in lieu of it.

17

that it represented. Probably it was because money was in an inert metal form that there was a great tendency to regard it as sterile. However, with the advent of paper money and particularly with the movement from the gold standard a new philosophy of money became inevitable and with it a new approach to usury or interest. Lewis Watt summarizes the eighteenth-century position of the Catholic Church relating to the uses of money as follows: 'To transfer to another the ownership of a sum of money on condition that a similar amount is returned after a certain time, but increased by a further sum as consideration for the right to use the money, is unjust and usurious.' Gradually, however, as sometimes happens, theology eventually adjusted to practice and current views. Little by little, the use of money and the margin of profit as compensation for allowing such use, was accepted.

First it was thought necessary for there to be trading purposes and an ensuing profit. It was a charge for risks—a kind of insurance against loss—or it would be in the translation of the money into property and the consequent charging of rent. All such uses were eventually regarded as permissible. As Adam Smith in *The Wealth of Nations* said: 'As something can everywhere be made by the use of money, something ought everywhere to be paid for the use of it.' Looking at the whole approach of the Roman Catholic Church to money, R. H. Tawney in *Religion and the Rise of Capitalism* said: 'The Papacy was, in a sense, the greatest financial institution of the Middle Ages, and as its fiscal system was elaborated, things became not better, but worse. The abuses which were a trickle in the 13th Century were a torrent in the 15th. . . . Priests, it is from time to time complained, engage in trade and take usury. Cathedral chapters lend money at high rates of interest. The profits of usury, like those of simony should have been refused by churchmen as hateful to God . . .'

All the reformers appear to have been against usury in the sense of extortionate interest, but some, particularly

Some past attitudes to money

John Calvin, appear to differentiate firmly between extortionate interest and reasonable interest, Calvin himself seeing nothing wrong in a reasonable return on capital that is lent. Particularly in the earlier years, the Church spoke with a divided voice on the use of money and it represents an uncertainty relating to the fundamental position of money in a Christian society.

Perhaps one day someone will seek to trace the influence of the celibate priesthood on the Church's theology on sex. The curious views which emanated from the medieval Church on this subject not only a striking attraction to a form of Gnosticism, but also represent a statement by those who had no direct experience of their subject. In a similar way, much of the medieval Church's theologizing on the use of money, which condemned the charging of interest on money lent, and regarded it as much a sin as murder or robbery, represented an ill-informed approach to the material world by those who were not experts in the field of finance.

Some of the old theological arguments regarding high interest rates have been superseded by modern problems of inflation. To maintain capital intact, with no element of charge, would need at least an interest figure equal to the rate of currency depreciation. Figures of 30 per cent at one point in 1976 would not have been unreasonable if they could have been obtained. With inflation at this rate an individual paying income tax at the standard rate would require a 45 per cent interest rate to keep his money intact, without any real gain. How some of the early Church divines would have coped with such a concept is not easy to see.

In the same way that nationally money does not have a life of its own but merely reflects external pressures, so at a personal level money reflects the personal priorities and philosophies of its owner. It is true that undue concentration on the accumulation of money appears to give the commodity a life of its own because it overwhelms the nature of the individual, but it is the love of, or even the lust for, money that is 'the root of all evil'.

The way a person deals with his money indicates in a sense the measurement of spiritual values accepted by that person and to a certain extent it also indicates the degree of spiritual maturity achieved by him. Jesus is recorded as saying in John's Gospel, 'I have come that men may have life, and may have it in all its fullness' (John 10:10). A Christian should have a philosophy of *real* enjoyment. Not for him the half-hearted pecking at life; he should aim to live in such a way that everything that occurs, every possession that he has, is savoured to the full. Whatever he has—a pleasant garden or a comfortable armchair—he enjoys it knowing that it is a gift from God and every moment of enjoyment teaches him something about God. In buying something new he savours in his purchase an increased excellence compared with the object that is replaced; his enjoyment might be through the aesthetic quality of the object or because of its usefulness, or even through the negative quality of delighting in the absence of an irritation caused by the malfunction of what it replaced.

A Christian who considers that he should go through life not acknowledging or noticing the material things in it, not only is missing much of life's treasure but also is turning his back on part of the riches of God's grace. It used to be considered by many in years gone by that the only enjoyment that the Christian should experience was the enjoyment of sacrifice and this was taken several stages further by some of the religious Orders that induced masochistic or even sadistic inflictions of pain in order, they believed, to associate themselves with the sacrifice of Jesus. Some of the extreme Puritans followed the same sour path of misery and joylessness in religion.

Of course, sacrifice and pain and suffering are all part of the Christian life and probably most would regard this element as a vitally important part of the Christian experience. For too long, however, a hesitancy has inhibited the full enjoyment of material things. The teaching of Jesus through example shows very clearly that he believed in enjoying the good things of life and was criticized by the ascetics of the time for doing so. 'For John came, neither eating nor drinking and they say, "He is possessed". The Son of Man came eating and drinking, and they say, "Look at him! a glutton and a drinker, a friend of tax-gatherers and sinners!" And yet God's wisdom is proved right by its results' (Matthew 11:18 f.).

There is a danger inherent in the philosophy of enjoyment because of an inbuilt urge in human nature to improve on whatever one has; to seek yet higher realms of enjoyment than is possessed at any given moment or to find some quicker way of achieving it. The whole weight of Christian teaching on the subject is that the religion induces a real enjoyment of things as they are, and does not set one running up an escalator of insatiable desire. One of the most dramatic illustrations of this aberration is the quest for perfection in Hi-Fi electronic equipment. No matter what equipment the enthusiast has, he can always see something that is better. Indeed, it is sometimes said that the enthusiast's ultimate enjoyment is to have his equipment on at full volume with a perfectly blank record and to hear nothing. Only then does he realize that his equipment has reached the zenith in his fight against hiss and rumble and other imperfections!

Looked at another way, the alert Christian quickly realizes that the last 10 per cent of improvement is achieved by paying the last 90 per cent in the price and he must therefore learn to savour to the full and enjoy to the full what is a reasonable balance between price and quality.

In his zest for living and enjoyment of material things there will be added zest for knowledge; because he finds life interesting and colourful he will want to learn more of the material world in which he lives, of people's attitude to it and relationships with it and with other people.

Christian emphasis on the enjoyment of the 'good things' of life is not a tragic relapse into Epicureanism. 'Eat, drink, and be merry, for tomorrow we die' is not Christian philosophy. There is all the difference in the world between the man who trains his palate to savour to the full a well-prepared meal with varied and exciting tastes, and the man who bolts down his wife's cooking without noticing what he is eating. The Christian is interested in quality, not quantity. The Epicurean sees disaster approaching and seeks to hide from its coming by excesses of all kinds.

Christian teaching on enjoyment of material things follows and develops the sturdy spirituality of the Old Testament interpreting the material world as good. For example, 'Be fruitful and increase, fill the earth and subdue it, rule over the fish in the sea, the birds of the heaven, and every living thing that moves upon the earth'. God also said: 'I give you all plants that bear seed everywhere on earth, and every tree bearing fruit which yields seed: they shall be yours for food. All green plants I give for food to the wild animals, to all the birds of heaven and to all reptiles on earth, every living creature.' And so it was and God saw all that he had made, and it was very good' (Genesis 1:28 ff.).

Even in the choice poetry of Isaiah 40 and its creation visions, although the majesty and the power of God is revealed as being so much vaster than that of man, who is likened to a grasshopper, the whole concept is that the earth, which is good, has been given to man to work in as a skilful craftsman, subject only to the over-riding power of God. Success and power in living is suggested as being contained in the ability to relate to God: 'Lift up your eyes to the heavens; consider who created it all' (Isaiah 40:26).

People can be very eccentric in the emphasis which they place on certain attitudes to money. For example, I once knew a millionaire who, whilst being extremely generous in the gifts of large sums of money and in lavish hospitality, always insisted that his guests paid for even local telephone calls they were obliged to make whilst on his premises. The more carefully one examines people's attitudes, including one's own, to money, the more one comes to the conclusion that they are riddled with inconsistencies. This makes it more important that money must never be allowed to dominate. It is the servant, and this is equally applicable to the fanatical entrepreneur who has no regard for anything except profits and the militant trade unionist seeking ever higher wages. Both are in danger of forfeiting not only the advantage of a pleasant working life but also any real achievement in the content of a spiritual value to life.

There are, in fact, a number of excesses in personal attitudes to money which can be regarded as against the spirit of the New Testament, and which banish the real enjoyment of things. For example, meanness can apply either to meanness to oneself or meanness to other people. It may denote a sickness of spirit that needs psychological investigation; or it may merely represent a certain attitude to life which has in time become more and more rigid. Occasionally old people, who were thought by neighbours to have been very poor, die, and when the house is entered after death, it is found that money is bursting out from under carpets, mattresses, and from many other recep-tacles and that all the time the person was very wealthy indeed. What could have been a relatively comfortable life became, through meanness, a masochistic experience of artificial poverty.

There are those who will not give a penny to help others but believe that everything they earn should be devoted to their own personal good and they will not even drop a ten pence piece in a charitable collecting box in the High Street. There are husbands who deny their wives sufficient money to maintain a reasonable standard of housekeeping or clothing for the family. Some people will not spend a penny on themselves and will delight in making their clothes last well beyond that point when the majority of people would have regarded them as fit only for the dust-bin—people indeed who resent every tiny piece of expenditure on anything at all. The question of not spending money becomes of supreme importance to them and dominates their whole outlook on life. Such people are soon noted by their contemporaries and are usually cordially disliked. Meanness may, of course, have been engendered by a genuine fear for the future or may have been initiated by a very unpleasant experience in the past, such as being unexpectedly out of work for a prolonged period and not wishing to be in a difficult position again. A miserly counting-up of accumulating assets (particularly if it is associated with a neurotic hoarding or worry about safeguards, or even the erosion of inflation on one's capacity to purchase items in the future) can induce the very antithesis of enjoyment and life becomes a misery.

This is the warning of the Sermon on the Mount: 'No, do not ask anxiously, "What are we to eat? What are we to drink? What shall we wear?" All these are things for the heathen to run after, not for you, because your heavenly Father knows that you need them all. Set your mind on God's Kingdom and his justice before everything else, and all the rest will come to you as well. So do not be anxious about tomorrow; tomorrow will look after itself. Each day has troubles enough of its own' (Matthew 6:31 ff.). Whilst this injunction is of direct application to only one form of meanness, much if not all incidences of this state could be eradicated by a genuine trust in God for they all derive from a sense of insecurity.

Even the most extreme form of meanness derives from the physiological drive which sustains men from extinction. It makes them self-reliant and able to look after themselves; it also engenders in its undisciplined form rapacity and an almost infinite capacity for trouncing one's fellows. This has been a sad part of the human scene since Old Testament times. It was comparatively easy, once a man had made the transition from an ordinary peasant to the possessor of certain assets, such as sheep and goats and possibly land, for him to become not only the master of other men, but also to make other men his slaves. From then onward, it was a short step for a class of the rich to be clearly identified as those who were not only wealthier than their fellows, but who were also avid to increase their wealth, even if this involved decreasing or even removing the minute assets of the poor. It is against such injustice that the prophets cry out with fierce denunciation; the most trenchant was Amos: 'You turn justice upside down and bring righteousness to the ground, you that hate a man, who brings the wrong-doer to court, and loathe him who speaks the whole truth: for all this, because you levy taxes on the poor and exhort tribute of grain from them, though you have built houses of hewn stone, you shall not live in them, though you have planted pleasant vineyards, you shall not drink wine from them. For I know how many your crimes are and how countless your sins, you who persecute the guiltless, hold men to ransom and thrust the destitute out of court' (Amos 5:7–12). Or again, in Amos 8:4 ff., 'Listen to this, you who grind the destitute and plunder the humble, you who say: "When will the new moon be over, so that we may sell our corn? When will the sabbath be past so that we may open our wheat again, giving short measure in the bushel and taking overweight in the silver, tilting the scales fraudulently, and selling the dust of wheat; that we may buy the poor for silver, and the destitute for a pair of shoes?''.'

Without doubt, much of the Old Testament prophets' message is a fulmination against the apostasy of Israel, but threaded throughout there is a concept of social justice, which is considered as part of the message and the desire of Jehovah whose very nature is righteousness.

A second way of banishing real enjoyment is by flashing around possessions in order to draw attention to one's self. If the enjoyment of material possessions is only found in demonstrating to others that one has them (adding, perhaps, the price paid!) then enjoyment is ephemeral because when people become less impressed and take little notice, the enjoyment disappears and one is left with something that to oneself has virtually no real value. There are so many scriptural injunctions which are directed against vanity that it is scarcely necessary to choose an example. The Christian depicted in the Sermon on the Mount is one who has no need to do things with a flourish of trumpets—to win the admiration of men (Matthew 6:2)—his happiness lies in being 'of a gentle spirit' which has the earth for his possession (Matthew 5:5); it is only those who have missed this pearl of great price that need to exaggerate themselves in order to find a brief happiness in admiring looks from others.

Allied to the spirit of vanity is the attitude of the spendthrift who is quite unable to retain money in his possession, and who as soon as payday arrives, has to go out and spend it. He may fritter his money stupidly by throwing money around in a pub, or he may spend it on different items that in themselves are useful but the purchase of them together makes for reckless expenditure representing far too high a proportion of total income. Such spending habits are often psychologically inspired. Frequently a spendthrift is a very vain person who tries to display a wealth which he does not possess, or attempts to ingratiate himself with those who otherwise would be unimpressed. Such a person who has to buy friendship often needs to borrow more than money before the next payday.

It is not always easy to decide whether a lifestyle becomes ostentatious merely because it is superior to that enjoyed by those round about. Frequently the motives of the person with the possessions need to be taken into account as well. For example, a man who has spent £1,000 in landscaping a small front garden in order to impress his neighbours is very different from the man who does the same thing because the only joy in life that his invalid wife has is to look out on a small part of earth that brings colour and beauty into an otherwise drab life. Where motive, especially secret motive, is an important part in the judgement of a person's attitude to life, it becomes very obvious that the teaching of Jesus against judging others ('Pass no judgement and you will not be judged. For as you judge others so you will yourselves be judged'—Matthew 7:1–2) is of supreme importance to a Christian, not only because it enables us to avoid making unfair judgements but because it releases us from one of the mainsprings of dissatisfaction, namely comparing ourselves and our possessions all the time with those that other people receive or possess. The flavour of enjoyment of our own possessions disappears when we are looking over our shoulder enviously at what others have—just as any enjoyment from a piece of music evaporates when another is played as loudly at the same time!

The third way in which real enjoyment can be banished is through a lust for domination. Money, and the power it brings, is often sought for the reason that it gives to the individual power over other people. Whilst it may be true that a person starting off with this intention might consider that in *his* hands the power that money brings can be used well and beneficially for other people, experience has shown that this initial altruism is often lost in the corrupting influence of power itself. This is because once power has been achieved, people are very reluctant to relinquish it, and partly because they enjoy, in a perverted way, throwing their weight about. They may also fear what others whom they injured in their search for power would do to them, if they themselves ever relinquished it.

Whilst it is comparatively easy to accept these observations, one needs to be careful concerning their implications. Entrepreneurial power and enterprise represented the mainspring of the present prosperity of this country and of the western world. No one is entirely pure in his motives, not even those who expressly seek to be so, and it clearly would not be of advantage to anyone if the goose that laid the golden egg was killed. Or, to put it a different way, if we so emasculated the thrust of production of wealth that it dropped to a trickle, we should not necessarily have thereby benefited mankind. Thus the Christian seeks to do two things. He tries to assess his own motives, so that he does not violate his high Christian standards and he also joins in attempts to provide what might be a lower legal framework for society to operate in so that at least a minimum code is achieved. He does not, however, seek to become a sort of financial Hercule Poirot, delving into other people's motives and actions, still less does he spawn gratuitous judgements unless what is done is flagrantly against the public good.

This, of course, begs the question as to whether the Christian is prepared to tolerate the capitalist system at all. The relative merits of that and the alternative system are dealt with later. As both are worked by fallible human beings, in each there are opportunities to dominate and oppress one's fellows, and one is back again with the warnings of Amos and others.

3 Living in an affluent world

A Christian has to come to terms with the affluent society. He can do this in two ways. He can reject it and seek to live the life of an ascetic or as near to it as he reasonably can; or, as we have been exploring, he can enjoy to the full the life that has been granted to him, within certain clearly defined limits which he himself learns to set.

Unfortunately, many Christians appear to succeed only in an uneasy compromise between the feeling for asceticism and the feeling for enjoyment: this results in a very negative and pallid approach to life that commends itself neither to the true ascetic nor to the extreme Epicurean.

A Christian often feels guilty when possessing something, in that he knows that there is someone who does *not* have it. This produces very often a muddled philosophy which more often than not involves sweeping under the carpet a whole series of questions that ought to be answered. We shall be examining later what rules should apply to the giving to others, but in the affluent world it is important that we should recognize the relationship which ideally should exist between one's capacity to earn, the savings that can be achieved, and what should be given to others.

John Wesley, in his well known forty-fourth sermon on the use of money, gives a penetrating analysis of the problem and some useful advice to those who live in a society which is somewhat simpler than our own. It would not be inappropriate to look at his teaching in some depth. He bases it on the parable of the Unjust Steward, using the text from Luke 16:9, 'I say unto you, make to yourselves friends of the mammon of unrighteousness; that, when ye fail, they may receive you into everlasting habitation'. He begins by criticizing Christians for not studying the use of money nearly enough, compared with those who are, 'men of the world'. Wesley makes the familiar (to us) distinction between the *love* of money being the root of all evil and the thing itself, stressing that the fault does not lie in money but in those who use it. The whole weight of the sermon is thrown on what are described as 'three plain rules'. One is, 'gain all you can'. The second is, 'save all you can', and the third is 'give all you can'.

The first rule is qualified by saying that in gaining all that is possible, it should be done, 'without buying gold too dear'. That is to say, it should not be achieved at the expense of life, or of health, reasonable food or sleep. It should not be gained in unhealthy employment, he says, and quotes one or two of those which were very unhealthy in those days—dealing too much with arsenic, and breathing air tainted with streams of melting lead.

Gain, Wesley maintained, should be achieved without hurting our minds as well as our bodies and that meant that it should not be done 'by robbing or defrauding the king of his lawful customs'. He even makes the distinction between those who can follow a particular activity or trade in perfect innocence and those who cannot. For example, he admits that he could not study, 'to any degree of perfection, either mathematics, arithmetic, or algebra, without being a Deist, if not an Atheist: and yet others may study them all their lives without sustaining any inconvenience'. A gain must be achieved without hurting our neighbour by damaging his material possessions (pawnbroking he excludes on the grounds that whatever good might be attempted 'all unprejudiced men see with grief to be abundantly overbalanced by the evil'). He begs the question as to what is a 'fair' price when he indicates that it would be wrong to sell goods below the market price and thus ruin his neighbour's trade. The gain must not hurt a neighbour's body, which would prohibit the sale of 'all that liquid fire, commonly called drams, or spirituous liquors'. Similarly, a neighbour's soul must not be damaged by our gain, so that in no way should a Christian pander either directly or indirectly to 'his unchastity or intemperance'. This apparently ruled out anything to do with 'taverns, victualling houses, opera houses, play houses or any other places of public, fashionable diversion'. Having made all these restrictions, Wesley emphasizes again the importance of gaining all that is possible by honest industry and diligence, losing no time, doing nothing carelessly, using common sense and all the understanding which God gives, learning from the experience of others to achieve an even greater degree of efficiency.

The second great rule is saving everything possible, so that all that is gained should not be wasted in pleasures of sin, by which he means not only gluttony and drunkenness but anything which panders to luxury, including 'gratifying the desire of the eye by superfluous or expensive apparel or by needless ornaments'. Similarly, money should not be spent to gain the admiration of others nor should it be spent on children, for fear that they will be led to enjoy the kind of luxury that you have learned to avoid. Again, children should not be left any money at all unless it was certain that they would use it well.

Wesley then passes on to his third great rule of giving all that is possible. He sees no point in obeying the first two and having no further use for the money than burying it in the earth. He admits it is necessary to provide necessities for one's self, for one's wife and family and servants (these last, curiously enough to modern listeners, are not considered luxuries). Next in order of priority are Church members, and finally, doing good to all men. Should there be any doubt as to whether expenditure is wise or necessary, there are a number of rules which can be applied: Is one acting in character as a Lord's steward? Is what is being done in obedience to the Scriptures? Can the expense be regarded as 'a sacrifice to God through Jesus Christ'? Is there likely to be a reward at the resurrection for the work?

He thinks it unlikely that further doubts should arise, but if it does, prayer remains the longstop. This can be achieved only by regarding God as the true owner and offering him not a tenth, or a third or a half, but *all* that is God's, managing God's gifts as both the Scriptures and our own consciences require.

In many ways it is not easy to fault the approach and the logic of Wesley. Certainly as far as the first rule is concerned, we need very little more except that our knowledge of psychology today makes it clear that there could be disadvantages in working so hard without a break or relaxation that our fundamental health is injured. Why this did not appear to be understood in Wesley's day it is difficult to say. Certainly the norm was of unremitting work required by all those in employment from very early hours in the morning until dark or after. There are many jobs that require this today and if the motivation is strong enough it is achieved and there are a number of people who are quite capable of working continuously over protracted periods—young housemen in our hospitals, for example. Nonetheless there are many who cannot sustain long spells of labour and it is necessary for each person to work out for himself how hard he can work. For the Christian therefore, the basic rule as set out by Wesley is still valid except that one would probably place rather more emphasis than Wesley did on the last word, 'work all you *can*'.

Protestants have traditionally viewed work with extreme seriousness, emphasizing the sinfulness of idleness, and finding it impossible to adopt a relaxed attitude to leisure. There are many ministers of religion today who not only refuse to have a regular day off a week, but who always feel guilty when they give themselves any time off at all. Not only is there a danger that their families suffer from neglect, but their own health can be affected by the dual effects of the long hours of work and a neurosis growing secretly through frustrated resentment at the lack of leisure. The Bible apparently has no co-ordinated view on work, and even if it had, it might not have helped too much in our attitude to modern production methods. In Genesis work is apparently regarded as a punishment.

'Because you have listened to your wife and have eaten from the tree which I forbade you, accursed shall be the ground on your account. With labour you shall win your food from it all the days of your life..

It will grow thorns and thistles for you, none but wild plants for you to eat.

You shall gain your bread by the sweat of your brow until you return to the ground' (Genesis 3:17 ff.).

The punishment is not negative, however, and from man's labour stems a future that is full of progress and even nobility.

A rather different attitude to work is found by implica-tion in the Ten Commandments (Exodus 20:8 ff.). The Sabbath day was to be regarded as separated to God. The implication here is not that work is a punishment from which one would escape at any opportunity, but something that requires a stern rule to keep one from continuing. The antecedents of the 'holy' day are difficult if not impossible to trace. It is clear that it was very different from a working day, it was one that was set apart for God—a joyful day, but not one of idleness. The concept develops throughout the Bible until by the time of Jesus the Sabbath was enmeshed in spiritually deadening rules, which Jesus deliberately broke himself and permitted to be broken (Matthew 12:1–14). The works of man should have a unity of pur-pose with those of God and too rigid a compartmentalizing of work and leisure (or the Sabbath) was erroneous.

The attitude of Jesus to work appears to be that it is an opportunity for exercising God's gifts; the more bestowed on one, the more is expected. Indeed, such concepts were not emphasized in the traditions of the age. Jesus teaches that man should exercise his talents in every way that is possible in order to achieve all he can and have an abundant life, 'I have come,' said Jesus, 'that men may have life, and they have it in all its fulness' (John 10:10). There is no suggestion in the teaching of Jesus that there is anything in the fulness of the earth to fear, or to induce guilt or in any way to inhibit the real enjoyment of life. It is, however, a philosophy that requires man to control his demands by a very careful watch on excess which can lead to greed.

Jesus exhorts his followers to use all means that they can, to gain from their personal exertions. This seems to be the nub of the parable of the pound (Luke 19:11 ff.) and of the parable of the talents (Matthew 25:14 ff.). There are dangers in allegorizing parables and of finding too many meanings within them, and it must be admitted that many parables might well have the purpose of exhorting Christ-ians to continue waiting for the second coming of Christ and of warning contemporary Jews against opposition to his Kingdom. Nonetheless, the emphasis and, indeed, the whole nature of the stories indicate a kind of human ac-tivity that is regarded as worthy and to be applauded.

Thus, to return to Wesley, probably a more balanced attitude to work is required, recognizing that it is the only way of producing real wealth from God's world.

Where one comes to a greater difficulty in understanding Wesley is in relation to his second rule. Here perhaps more than anywhere the differences of time are apparent. The extreme frugality of Wesley which required no ornament, nothing beautiful or colourful, seems to be very much out of accord with our current thinking. Wesley, of course, had some very peculiar ideas, as did many people in those days about many things, particularly with regard to children. The rules which applied to the education of children at Kingswood, if they are studied, indicate something of a nightmare for children; with no holidays, hardly any break from work, extreme rigours and what might appear to us quite unnecessary frugality. The rules of the school by any standard must be regarded today as intolerable. For example, the General Rules of the House laid down:

Living in an affluent world

First, the Children rise at Four, Winter and Summer, and spend the Time till Five in private: Partly in Reading, partly in Singing, partly in Self-examination or Meditation (if capable of it) and partly in Prayer. They at first use a short Form (which is varied continually) and then pray in their own Words.

Secondly, At Five, they attend the Publick Service. From Six they work till Breakfast. For as we have no Play-Days (the School being taught every Day in the Year but Sunday) so neither do we allow any Time for Play on any Day. He that plays when he is a Child, will play when he is a Man.

On Fair Days they work, according to their Strength in the Garden; on Rainy Days in the House. Some of them also learn Music: And some of the larger will be employed in Philosophical Experiments. But particular Care is taken that they never work alone, but always in the Presence of a Master.

We have six Masters in all; One for teaching French, Two, for Reading and Writing, and Three for the Ancient Languages.

Thirdly, The School begins at Seven, in which Languages are taught 'till Nine, and then Writing, etc. 'till Eleven. At Eleven the Children walk or work. At Twelve they dine, and then work or sing 'till One. They diet thus: . . .

Then follow what today would seem a most frugal and unappetising series of meals.

From One to Four Languages are taught, And then Writing, etc. 'till Five. At Five begins the Hour of Private Prayer. From Six they walk and work 'till Supper. A little before Seven the Publick Service begins. At Eight they go to bed, the youngest first.

Charles Wesley summed up the view in the following verse:

> Let heathenish boys
> In their pastimes rejoice,
> And be foolishly happy at play:
> Overstocked if they are,
> We have nothing to spare,
> Not a moment to trifle away.

One suspects that the harshness of this attitude to work is also seen in the question of saving all that one can. There is in Wesley no suggestion that the world in which we live is one to be enjoyed, and that if we work hard enough God is prepared to allow us to enjoy, at least partly, the fruits of our labours.

Even if one accepts almost completely Wesley's first rule, the problem for the Christian in the twentieth century in applying his third rule is to achieve a correct balance between current expenditure and current giving, taking into account that saving for the future or a rainy day is, apart from a necessary reserve for house repairs or some other emergency, often taken care of by sophisticated pension arrangements. With heavy taxation during life and other duties applicable after death, the leaving of money to one's heirs has become more unlikely and less desirable. If one has achieved a certain success in a business, however, and believes that one's children will be able to manage and run the business successfully to the benefit of the community after one's death, it is clearly a good thing to seek to leave them this opportunity. For many the mere passing on of wealth is not necessarily an advantage. Full education enables children to enter almost any profession they are capable of entering, and this is the greatest legacy that can be passed to the next generation, second only to the pleasure that they themselves will experience in achieving their heart's desire once the opportunity is given them. The leaving of too much money by a father or mother has often led to very considerable trouble and has many times led to the ruin of a character that would perhaps, with the spur of relative poverty, have reached considerable achievement.

The criteria to be used in establishing a balance between current expenditure and current giving is not easy to determine, and is complicated by the further question how far one should accept surrounding lifestyle as the norm. If your neighbour considers something a necessity, does it necessarily mean that you should, also? One of the problems for the Christian is that yesterday's luxuries very soon become today's necessities; more rarely, in a curious way, yesterday's necessities in some instances become today's luxuries. For example, as with Wesley, a hundred or more years ago any educated person would consider themselves very badly off indeed if they were not in a position to employ at least one servant, but today even people with comparatively good jobs find it very difficult to afford anyone to do more than intermittent housework. Perhaps this is one reason why yesterday's luxuries, the washing machine and refrigerator, are becoming more and more necessities.

A wife going out to work might be the result of a desire for a higher lifestyle, but then what is often regarded as a higher lifestyle becomes a necessity because she has no time to do many of the things that she would have done had she been at home all the time. For example, she perhaps no longer has time to make jams and marmalade as her mother did, but instead she has a freezer and when she makes a meat pie or a jam tart, she might make half a dozen and freeze them, to be ready for later use, thus saving a great amount of time when she comes to prepare the next hurried meal on returning home from work. Similarly the clearing up after meals is facilitated by a dishwasher.

Twenty years ago, to have two cars was considered excessive. Nowadays when a wife has to travel to a job and public transport is not practicable, and when her husband also needs a car for his job, a second car becomes a necessity. To the extent that her job may be just as much of service to the community as his, there appears to be every Christian justification for the possession of this 'tool for her work'. Once again, however, it appears that the question of motive or reason is of importance in coming to any ethical judgement of the issue. If the chosen second car was to be, say, a coupé with a folding roof—a luxurious alternative to an ordinary saloon car—it would be unnecessarily luxurious.

One hundred years ago a continental 'grand tour' was the fortune of only those who were very well off. Today most manual workers, if they are reasonably competent in managing their budgets, are able, if they so desire, to pay for a package tour of Switzerland or even further afield. The motive and the approach to any particular holiday can determine whether it is unnecessarily luxurious. A month touring Africa to someone who needs to study life in other countries and will use accumulated knowledge to the advantage of themselves and Africans, might be no extravagance. Even someone gaining as much pleasure and knowledge as possible from a package holiday would be less wasteful than someone who had a week of excesses in Southend-on-Sea.

What seems to be quite obvious is that there is no point in having various material things and using current resources and feeling guilty about them.

Just as we learn to savour to the full such material possessions as we have, so at the same time we should learn not to become so attached to them that it matters if they are taken away. In other words, at all times the Christian should be the master of material things and not be mastered by them. This is sometimes defined theologically as recognizing that we are only stewards of God's things and not absolute owners. Because of his enjoyment of what he has, the Christian is content; he is not always lusting for more and better. As Paul says, ' . . . I have learned to find resources in myself whatever my circumstances. I know what it is to be brought low, and I know what it is to have plenty. I have been very thoroughly initiated into the human lot with all its ups and downs—fullness and hunger, plenty and want. I have strength for anything through him who gives me power' (Phillipians 4:11–13).

Many people have serious difficulties through bad personal organization. The discoveries of Mr Micawber are well known. It may be that in some instances overspending is due to a feckless indifference to money available, but

Living in an affluent world

often it is caused by bad budgeting. Even the poorest find it is possible to have a small reserve to meet an emergency, and it does not require much imagination or effort to plan ahead so that anticipated expenditure meets available income. It requires rather more discipline to implement and adhere to the budget, but the smaller the income the more important the task becomes.

A clear budget simplifies the task of assessing what is available to give away, although there are other factors in giving which need to be considered. To these we now turn.

To put Christian giving under the microscope of close analysis is, in a sense, an impertinence, for it is a spontaneous action and as soon as there is calculation or query or reservation it becomes less than a full-blooded symbol of our recognition that others are brothers in Christ and children of the same Father. Probably every Christian at some time or other will give more than a reasonable assessment would consider prudent. When confronted with a dramatic situation, the death of a colleague for example, contributions to assist his wife become urgent and personal. One does not stop to think how much one should give. What is available is immediately handed over.

Even this spontaneity, especially when related to more normal acts of giving, tends to have its limitations. In certain circumstances it can lead to what Christian Stewardship directors in post-second-world-war campaigns used to call, 'loose change giving'—one's gifts to God were based on the accident of loose change, deriving from previous transactions in purse or pocket. In these circumstances one never took a coherent and systematic look at the place of giving in relation to the whole of one's income. Thus, although in certain emotional moments people might be induced to give comparatively large sums, when taken overall on an annual basis the amounts given may not be particularly creditable. We all tend to think we give rather more away than in fact we do.

There are two major questions which need to be answered. The first is, 'How much shall we give?', and the second is, 'How shall we assess priorities in giving?'. It is, however, impossible to give definitive answers to these questions. To start with, the amount of available cash will depend very much on the income received. Not only is it true that the less income a person has, the less he has available for gifts, but also that the higher proportion of his smaller income needs to be spent on the necessities of life. The larger income a person has, the greater the range there is of possible choice of purchases. However, this spread is often severely restricted by circumstances and even social conventions and pressures. A man with £10,000 a year before tax, for example, might appear to have a substantial income available compared with a man having £5,000 a year, but once taxation has taken its share the difference is considerably narrowed. Tradition also often imposes on the better-off parents an obligation to provide their children with an expensive education such as they had themselves, and by the time they have paid for one or two sons or daughters at private schools there is not that much left over for giving away. (How far one has an absolute moral right to use one's income in this particular way is the subject of lively debate in itself; but many people would think it reasonable that a person, if he does place such a high value on private education, should attribute even a sacrificial portion of his own income to his children's well-being. It could be argued that a better education means that children stand a better chance of a higher standard of living at a later date and that therefore they also are in a better position, not only to create wealth, but to give wealth to those who are in need—unless they, too, in their turn, decide to dedicate very high proportions of their income to private education for their children! There are, of course, those who maintain that private education brings a child an unfair advantage over others and should not be indulged in by Christians—but that is not the present subject.)

The Biblical policy of giving away a tenth of one's income is one simple solution to the problem of how much. It is followed by many today, but not in mainstream Christianity. It is favoured by some non-conformists and fundamentalist sects. It could be argued that with an employee's 6 or 7 per cent deduction for Social Security, plus 10 per cent from the employer, the poor and ill are supported by the whole of the community in a logical and systematic way. This may have superseded at least part of the tithe. Further consideration of this kind of giving will be found later in the context of other ways of supporting the Church and the needy.

No doubt it would be possible to devise sophisticated 'tax tables' for guidance of Christian giving, but not only would these be extremely unpopular, they would become too much of an automatic relinquishment of income and the donor would experience nothing of the true Christian spirit of giving. Thus in the end giving always comes down to personal judgement; it relates the feeling of gratitude one has to God, to the needs of others and our own personal affairs and circumstances. We cannot make judgements for others. One can only trust that one's conscience is sufficiently sharp to ensure that a reasonable proportion of all that we earn is passed on to those in need. Some consideration could be given to the use of a valued Christian friend or friends to assist 'from outside' in ensuring that one is giving adequately. The old Methodist Class Meeting, which readily discussed all practical problems, undoubtedly considered this one, too. It was reported by members of his congregation that a minister, an ex-missionary who had been shocked by the contrast between standards of living in the Far East and a London suburban area, scrutinized his congregation every Sunday for evidence of new items of clothing. If he found a woman with a new frock on, he solemnly chastised her, indicating that there were those in the world who had much greater need of the money she had spent on this unnecessary luxury! Not unnaturally, the minister's actions were severely resented by the congregation. Even if he had been right, it is clear that no one has the authority to judge for another what should be spent on one's self and what should be spent on others. There seems to be evidence that suggests that the older people get, the better they become at judging themselves. Whether it represents a growing maturity in the Christian faith or a growing sensitivity to the needs of others or a lessening of one's own needs, it is difficult to determine, but many ministers are of the opinion that the most generous members of their congregation are those on a pension.

People often say that one cannot judge what one should give until one has first assessed the need; it is only then that one can make a valid judgement on how great a priority that particular need should receive in the disposal of one's income. In so far as one's personal giving could never alleviate all the starvation in the world, the direct answer to this particular question is that the need is infinite and therefore there should be no restriction on one's giving for that reason. This applies, however, to everyone who has an income showing a surplus over absolute necessity and probably this in turn represents something like 90 per cent of the western world. It clearly would not be reasonable to expect everyone in the western world to give every penny above what is necessary for survival—such a theoretical policy would, if allowed, cause the collapse of the western economy and ultimately would benefit no one. It must be accepted, therefore, that there is a limit to what the generous Christian should give, which in turn suggests that whilst one has a responsibility to give on one's own behalf one does not have a moral requirement to give on behalf of others what is their share of the same responsibility.

One important question that needs to be answered in the wider question of priorities, is 'how far has a Christian the responsibility of ensuring, or seeking to ensure, that those in the third world have more than is sufficient to keep them alive?'. Even to ask the question seems harsh and hard-hearted, and probably at a personal level it would be entirely reprehensible. Yet if one accepts that God wishes all born into the world to stay alive, the rich nations have a responsibility to ensure that starvation is eradicated. Some might contend, however, that Christian duty (as opposed to Christian generosity) ends at that point. Provided a man has enough to eat and is living in a community of those who have a similar standard of living, does he need any further material aid to ensure that there is no impediment to his ability to come to terms with God's world and to extract from the experiences of life what God wishes him to extract? Judgements are always comparative. Little children running about barefoot in the African bush or in southern Italy might appear to be very poor indeed compared to those living in the wealthy suburbs of the capitals of rich nations, yet it is doubtful whether the children in wealthier environments are any happier, and indeed there is some evidence to suggest that their parents are less happy than the parents of those who are poor and that comparative wealth brings with it a lessening rather than an increasing pleasure in life. Therefore, it could be argued that wealth as such, once it has passed the poverty line, neither contributes to nor detracts from one's ability to be as God wants us. If this is so, it could be argued that theoretically it is the duty of the Christian to do no more than to seek to remove starvation and sow the seeds of an educative process which will enable the poor nations to grow wealthier and to educate themselves with such assistance as they themselves feel appropriate. Whilst that may be the cold logic of the situation, it can never satisfy the sensitivities of the Christian who feels a strong impulse to share. There is a further problem related to a coldly logical approach; social crowding and poor environment often bring disease and this requires the standard of living of all people to be raised considerably if not constantly. This might be answered by arguing that even in the western world there is not enough money to pay for medical refinements which are necessary to health but which the country cannot afford. Kidney machines in this country are a case in point.

The development in world communications has had its

impact on the situation also. The world has become a much smaller place. A hundred years ago it was considered to be a Christian duty to support intrepid missionaries to hack their way through the jungle to preach the Gospel and possibly, in the process, to donate food and medical supplies which demonstrated 'God's love' and the affection of their better-off brothers. At home, one provided soup and second-hand clothes to those living in the darkest slums of the cities. For the wealthy, this involved writing a cheque, and for the poorer it meant a halfpenny in the missionary box. Today, the starving in India and elsewhere are as prominent to the eye and as uncomfortable to the conscience as were the poor in the east end of London in William Booth's day. It is, however, no longer tolerable to purchase, by a few coppers in a charity box, vicarious alleviation of guilt through the activities of a few scattered individuals. The great stream of information about the Third World has alerted Christians as never before to the needs of those in distress, particularly those in the starvation areas, or those affected by earthquake or hurricane or other natural catastrophe. Organisations such as Christian Aid and Oxfam have prospered and received at least some help from the general public and rather more from Church members.

In our own country, local poor are largely taken care of by the Welfare State and even they are rich compared with most people in Africa, Asia and South America. Those in developing countries are expanding their industries with excruciating slowness, but at the same time they are naturally developing appetites for the good things of life, like everyone else. Compared with those in the richer countries, however, they grow poorer and their wanting will not have much waiting taken out of it in the foreseeable future.

There are many problems associated with organizations which seek to help the Third World and many questions are asked which as yet have not been fully answered. Organizations which have been very closely associated with

Christian Churches in the Third World and which distribute relief through the Churches probably have the most effective arrangements to ensure that those really in need receive what is given, but there are many tales of corruption, of goods mouldering in warehouses or side-tracked into the possession of those who put them on the Black Market, to make one feel uneasy about mass attempts to alleviate distress. The fact that someone in England is well-disposed to a poor man 5,000 miles away does not necessarily mean that that poor man's neighbour only 5 miles away is similarly disposed. A great danger, of course, is that these stories are sufficient to stop many people from giving at all and even an occasional exposure of a degree of inefficiency within a relief organization is sufficient to deter the unwilling from finding even a few pence to help.

There must always be fire brigade exercises bringing emergency relief and it is necessary for those involved in such exercises to ensure that opportunities to syphon off the goods or to use them corruptly are reduced to a minimum. Increasingly, however, relief agencies are coming to the conclusion that such exercises must be for a limited duration and must be supplemented, and eventually replaced, by exercises to educate those in need to help themselves. Rather than send a constant supply of grain to a household that is on the verge of starvation, it is much better to teach the family how to farm their small area of ground productively; to instruct them on the correct application of fertilizer and to enable them to collaborate with their fellows to devise an efficient system of irrigation so that their lands become far more fertile. Not only is this more effective in the long run, it also ensures a much higher degree of dignity and self-reliance in those receiving help.

A wealthy nation needs to establish a balance between the share of its wealth which is given away and that which is devoted in its own area to producing more wealth. Only a nation which continues to prosper will be able to continue to share its wealth. Too high a proportion given today might mean too small a proportion given in a year or two's time.

Just as it is believed by most people in this country that medical services are much better supplied by the State than by voluntary relief agencies, world poverty, or at least hunger, can be better alleviated by the wealthy nations of the world at Government level. Christian generosity is not merely a question of digging deep into the pocket or hand-bag, it is also exercised by badgering governments, often in an organized way, to ensure that national provision is made for the needy of other nations. There are also occasions where the Christian should have much more interest in the cartels formed by rich governments which depress the price of raw materials supplied by Third World countries. A fair price for sugar or cocoa, for example, would achieve far more than millions of pounds of special aid.

Unfortunately, what it is politically expedient for a government to give usually ensures that there is no danger of a wealthy nation exceeding the limit of what it ought to give! At the present time, the majority of countries giving well below 1 per cent of their gross national product are in danger of being mean to the point of disgrace. Our own country gives only half of the United Nations target of 0.7 per cent and is well down the league of giving for wealthier nations.

Related to this issue of giving and Christian responsibility is the whole question of the deprivation of future generations by our present greedy consumption of scarce resources. How can we make pious noises about generosity and giving to those in need, if we are squandering what may be regarded as belonging to others? Oil, for example, at the present rate of consumption will not last long into the twenty-first century. The difficulty about making a Christian judgement on this question is that many of the facts are not known. How big will future populations of the world be? Will they continue to grow or will they be decimated by nuclear war? Will birth control become very strict and reduce the numbers living on earth? Can we be sure that what we are needing now will be required in future? All kinds of energy possibilities are looming—the harnessing of waves and tides, solar energy, further developments in nuclear power stations, to name a few. Previous generations greatly denuded the earth of timber by using it for fuel, furniture and building construction—not to mention our own consumption of paper. It is difficult to say that the shortage of both soft and hard woods has proved a great hardship to the present generation, which has found other and cheaper materials to replace wood.

As far as future generations are concerned the Christian has a responsibility, but one that is limited by the distance we can see. An arbitrary cut-back now of, say, a huge percentage of oil consumption, besides being politically impossible, would not only mean very serious hardship for many millions, but certain starvation for millions more. Future events might demonstrate that the sacrifice was unnecessary.

Wasteful uses of resources are, however, another matter. Burning of North Sea gas, which is a by-product of oil production because it is not economically viable to do anything else with it, is a case in point. Driving large cars when smaller ones would do the same job is another.

What judgements future generations will make on ours is difficult to say. It is possible, but not certain, that they will be sharp, especially if they need to scavenge through our rubbish dumps, or even with processes as yet unknown, reclaim from the outer atmosphere materials we carelessly burned.

The second major problem relating to giving concerns the methods to be adopted in assessing priorities. There are so many voices appealing (with or without the help of professional fund-raisers) for those in need at home and abroad, that it is not easy to determine who needs help most.

Giving to others

A Christian approach might take the following into account:

(a) The alleviation of hunger or the effects of natural catastrophe have an elemental and immediate claim that is virtually impossible to resist.

(b) Requests for gifts to assist work in various areas in this country must be given varying priorities. There are charities directly involved in the treatment of suffering, those seeking to provide a more tolerable life for the handicapped and under-privileged, those involved in research: the long term, the short term, the helpful, the essential—all have their place. A measured judgement of the value of one as against another is virtually impossible. Personal preference, even if stimulated by emotion, must be given some freedom.

(c) There is seldom an 'either-or' choice. Money available can be spread over several causes or individuals.

(d) Care should be taken to ensure not only that the organization to be assisted is reputable, but also that it is efficient in achieving its aims. For example, Church charities often not only have lower administration costs, but are frequently better able to reach those in need. Using local churches and clergy in disaster areas often ensures that help is not deflected nor delayed.

(e) Appeals to help individuals in this country often need to be treated with great caution. There is a professsional class of beggar which uses remarkable plausibility. Recognition of this makes it more difficult to assist the genuine case. Giving assistance in kind, e.g. the provision of accommodation or food rather than cash, is one way to counter the rogues who go from minister to minister with tales of imaginary disasters which are supposed to have happened to them.

(f) In the context of a world of suffering, giving to one's dependent children poses great difficulty, particularly if they want things the parent considers they do not need. A

49

child deprived of things others have, because his parents have given elsewhere, might eventually grow into an adult who will never give. Whilst charity begins at home, however, it does not, for the Christian, mean a thoughtless indulgence of spoilt children. The parents may have a difficult mental balancing act to perform before they arrive at the right decision.

The permutations for considering priorities in all aspects of giving are limitless and personal. The experiences and temperament of the donor affect his judgement; from a Christian point of view this is normal and acceptable. Only if prejudice intervenes to blur his choice is condemnation justified. Only the individual concerned, and perhaps not even he, is in possession of all the knowledge necessary to make a judgement. It therefore follows that one is never warranted in criticizing the choice made by others in their giving. What they do might seem strange to us, but that is a matter between them and God.

5 Unearned wealth

Gambling and Speculation

Nonconformist denominations have spoken fairly firmly against gambling, not so much because of the danger of suddenly acquiring wealth to which one perhaps was not entitled, but because the principle of trying to get something for nothing was regarded as reprehensible. It was further believed that the process of longing to win, even with a very small outlay, was corrupting even if only mildly so. The Roman Catholic Church on the whole does not appear to have shared these views, and the Anglican Church has varied according to whether the particular parish was nearer the Roman Catholic or nonconformist wing of the Church.

The nonconformist conscience of the nineteenth and early-twentieth centuries has proved a valuable contributor to the total morality of the country, although there is evidence that there has been some exaggeration and even fanaticism about the stance of some. Some might consider the extreme teetotalism of the early twentieth-century Methodists a case in point, and the manner in which the Methodist Church has sought to eradicate even the slightest trace of chance from its activities (for example, guessing the number of peas in a bottle at a sale of work) hardly suggests a completely balanced view on the subject.

It is difficult to believe that someone who contributes a few 10p coins in an effort to support a charity raffle is in danger of having his mind or soul corrupted any more than the person who, for amusement, places small sums on the Derby or Grand National. Indeed, it might almost be suggested that a person who demonstrated a petty fanaticism and makes mountains out of other people's innocent molehills is in danger of corruption himself. Corruption comes from one's attitude to these activities and one has a suspicion that possibly it has much more to do with the attitude to life than to a particular single event or activity. For example, the person who has grave tendencies towards greed is just as likely to be corrupted in his business activities as he is in minor gambling. None the less, it is clear that the illness of the uncontrolled gambler is as serious as that of the alcoholic, and the argument that if you do not start it you will not suffer from it is unanswerable in its logic—indeed, it is just as logical as saying that if you do not drive a car you will not kill someone through careless driving.

The important thing, therefore, for the Christian is that he does *not need* to engage in the practice. He does not need it for excitement, because his life is adventurous already. He does not need to do it in an attempt to get more money because he can manage with what he already possesses. The likelihood of the Christian in these circumstances being confronted suddenly with unexpected winnings is small indeed.

A close psychiatric study on the processes of fanaticism might be interesting, but in many if not all of us there is a degree of benevolent fanaticism which needs watching. It is fatally easy to enter the process in defence of a genuine principle. The more analytical one becomes in examining a practice like gambling the more one tends to widen the examination area to discover 'impurities' which in turn are magnified if not distorted to appear more important than they are. In the post-war fear of Communism in America, minor youthful flirtation with Communism was magnified by McCarthyism to be a crime against the State. Christians in the past have operated in the same way, leading to the Inquisition for example.

Christian judgement on money matters, as in other things, must not be distorted by the elevation of trivia to take equal place with the really important. Methodists in

Unearned wealth

the past may have lost great opportunities for leadership in issues like gambling, simply because they tried to follow the scent of 'impurity' to absurd lengths. There are many very important problems to solve, like the regulation of the gambling industry, the corruption of individuals by the gambling scene, and the study of compulsive gambling. Compared with such problems, a witch hunt against games of chance in a church hall appears a foolish irrelevance.

Various forms of speculation provide an alternative method of making large gains—and perhaps even larger losses. 'Playing' the Stock market, gambling heavily on commodity prices altering in a given direction, property speculation particularly before the State clamped down, are all ways in which an element of skill is added to a large amount of luck to produce large and unreasonable profits. It is not always easy to determine where proper practice ends and speculation begins, but there are two criteria which help. One is the relationship between the degree of luck required and the amount of skill, knowledge and research which has gone into a business deal. The latter should always be the dominant factors, although it must be admitted that it is not possible to eliminate an element of luck from this, or any other aspect of human activity. The second is the motive which spurs a person to deal as he does. If he regards himself as a fair trader, seeking a reasonable profit in return for his activities, he can be separated from the 'whizz kid' who is out for a quick 'kill'.

Bequests

There are other ways in which surprise money might appear, the most likely being through a bequest. The bequest an individual will be most likely to receive is a house, or part of it, willed by his parents. For many people, however, the amount left by parents may not be more than a few hundred pounds—scarcely sufficient to pay for the funeral expenses. Occasionally, however, unexpected windfalls occur and whereas sometimes people are quite

53

clear what should happen to the money, on other occasions there is uncertainty. There seems to be no reason to suppose that it is wrong to accept for one's own personal use, or that of the family, assets deriving from a bequest. Jesus appears to accept this as normal behaviour in the introduction to the parable of the Prodigal Son (Luke 15:12 ff.).

The trouble comes in the rare instances where it is so sizeable as to alter the lifestyle of the individual and this is also the problem about large 'pools' wins. Quite apart from the fact that the recipient of such income is often besieged by many people who beg for help, some genuine, some not, he is equally sought after by long lost friends who always meant to get into contact and never did. There are many examples of lives being totally ruined by a sudden switch to a lifestyle to which the person is not accustomed and for which he has not been prepared. On a number of occasions pools winners have, looking back, wished they had never received a quarter of a million pounds or whatever it was. The first flush of excitement at being able to buy what one wants when one wants it is soon replaced by a boredom that deepens into a cynicism. One can never be sure of one's friends, how many of them are after one's money; having so much and ultimately doing so little makes relationships very difficult and there are many instances of marriages being broken because of quarrels over money which would never have occurred had the accustomed lifestyle been continued.

This is not to say that in every instance disaster is bound to happen. Some people have certainly kept their heads and used the money that has come by way of a bequest sensibly, perhaps by continuing a family business successfully or possibly using the capital to branch out into business on their own account—something which they had always dreamt of doing but had never been able to. Those that have their priorities clear in normal times are usually better able to adjust their lifestyle sensibly when abnormal circumstances arise. There seems to be no formal policy

Unearned wealth

which the Church should adopt in such instances. If it is right to argue that the Christian should sit loosely on the whole matter of wealth, it is equally true that he must feel under no compulsion to act in a certain way if and when any sudden wealth appears. A compulsion to spend such money rashly, or an irrational desire to hoard, can equally affect his personality. Large in his consideration should be, 'what can be done with the unexpected money for the benefit of the community as a whole'. If he himself can deploy it to produce wealth which will be for the benefit of others as well as himself, this is good. If he cannot, then consideration should be given to passing on at least a proportion to those who can. And here lies the fundamental problem. One of the most difficult things in the world is to give money away, especially sizeable sums. This is partly due to the uncertainty of life, whereby the majority of people feel they would not wish to prejudice their position in years to come by what might later appear to be a momentary impulse; and so they hold on, and then all the dangers which derive from the possession of wealth often begin to emerge.

It is an extraordinary thing that the Church which has a powerful message to speak to the world has remained comparatively quiet over the whole question of inflation. Part of the trouble is that this latest inflationary problem has come upon us relatively slowly in that the rate, initially very slow after the war, suddenly swelled to alarming proportions in the mid-seventies. Further, the ramifications of inflation are so complicated that few feel competent to speak about them; those that do usually disagree!

One of the greatest problems about inflation is not so much its monetary significance, although this is important enough; its effect on the individual is even more important in that it is a destroying and insidiously corrupting influence on a person's character. Psychologically, what happens is that it induces a sense of insecurity. As no one likes seeing his standards of living eroded, the faster the erosion takes place the more frantic the individual becomes in seeking to ensure that he himself is not left behind. When the inflation rate is around the 5 per cent per annum a good trade union leader will ensure that his workers are not unduly affected and will eventually make up for the erosion. He is not, however, looking all the time over his shoulder to see how other people are getting on. When the rate gets over the 20 per cent mark there is a headlong Gadarene rush over the precipice. Not only does he want to ensure that he recoups the 20 per cent that has taken place, he is peering anxiously over his shoulder to see if anybody is getting more, and if he sees or thinks he sees somebody doing better he wants yet more still. There is thus engendered such a state of tension and naked greed that the whole fabric of organized life is put at risk.

Far more severe is the animosity which grows up between employer and employee and between one group of workers and another and between workers and Government. Almost every section of the community thinks that it is badly treated and almost every group of workers believes itself to be a special case requiring special treatment.

Faced with such a situation the Church ought to have something more than pious platitudes to utter. Given a standard of living many times higher than is necessary actually to sustain life, the Christian believes that in Western civilization at the present day people are well able to survive on a very much lower standard of living, though few would find this acceptable. In the light of this belief the Christian attitude to an erosion in times of inflation is likely to be far less severe than the reaction of those who regard material things as their only treasure. One aspect of the message of the Church must therefore be the encouragement of a sense of balance. It must indicate that although reasonable steps must be taken to ensure (if this is possible without injuring others) that one's standard of living is not jeopardized, the churchman does not join in the mad attempt to secure more and more, resorting to all the crudity of jungle life in order to achieve such an end.

Further, the Church must speak up fearlessly in favour of the poor and helpless and this applies not only to the socially deprived but to those who do not belong to really powerful unions. There are so many groups of workers who, if they went to ultimate lengths, could reduce the delicate machinery of our present economic system to a smouldering chaos. Attention is paid to what the strong say, but much less attention is paid to the needs of those who, if they stop work in the pursuit of a pay claim, would not be noticed very much at all, and whose action certainly would carry no economic peril for others. If the national policy is every man for himself and every group for themselves and the Devil take the hindmost, then we are very soon to have a new rich and a new poor. The Church must stand up for fairness as between groups of workers. A great deal of positive and visionary thinking needs to be done on the whole question of reasonable reward. The Church has not pronounced on this with any degree of effectiveness.

What should determine whether a man is paid highly? Is a pop-star or a captain of industry 'worth' £100,000 per annum to the community? Does extra training entitle a man to extra emolument? If a doctor becomes a famous surgeon should he be entitled to fees which take him to the pop-star class? What compensation over and above a normal range should be paid to the miner who endures a lifetime of labour in the extreme darkness and dirt of the coalmine? Should anything extra be paid to the refuse collector, who not only has a heavy and uncomfortable physical task to perform, but one which is accompanied by a constant smell which would put most of us off our food for months? Should a job which is found to be very self-satisfying and interesting be paid less than one which is repetitive and boring? All these are crucial issues to which the Church should be directing itself, for in an inflationary era a more coherent and ethically and religiously balanced attitude is essential if some form of sanity is to return to the realm of wage bargaining and wage settlement.

It is possible to be idealistic about remuneration and maintain that the jobs that give the greatest satisfaction should be rewarded least, and work that is unrewarding in any other way should receive financial compensation. These, however, are clearly ideals of perfection and would be most difficult indeed to translate into practice.

One of the problems, of course, is that although possibly the majority of people might, for example, find that being a doctor is very interesting and rewarding, there will always be a certain percentage that find it very harrowing, worrying or very tiring. It would not be possible to reward the latter at a greater level than others doing the same job, merely because they got less satisfaction out of it. Further, satisfaction is an imprecise condition and one that varies in many people in accordance with their mood. Two other factors are important. One is the problem that many of the jobs generally most rewarding are those that require very considerable training. If one is to take away the rewards for this training, then it is by no means certain that the necessary number of people would apply for entrance into that particular occupation. The other is that such jobs are frequently internationally in demand. Human nature being what it is, if rewards are reduced in one country many thus affected will emigrate to another.

None the less, it does seem at least superficially, reasonable that higher taxation should not only be levelled at those who earn the greatest amount of money but that some fiscal recognition might be possible on the basis of a slightly higher taxation for certain occupations because of the pleasantness or satisfaction which is generally obtained in them. More easy to implement would be some fiscal benefit supplementing incomes in certain jobs that are singularly unpleasant and unrewarding, putting up the rate for such a job. For example, refuse collecting, which is hard, heavy work, often in inclement weather, could be a candidate for more favourable taxation. In the event, however, such jobs are very often done by those who can do no other and are often poorly paid. The matter is further complicated by the fact that sometimes those with limited intellectual gifts prefer boring jobs which would make some scream, simply because they learn to do them automatically and can chatter happily with those similarly working near by. Many repetitive jobs fall into this category.

Of course, the question of tax is often forgotten when the matter of high salaries is taken into account. We often talk of it being thoroughly wrong for the chairman of a very large company to receive, say, £100,000 per annum when an ordinary worker is earning as little as £3,000 or £4,000 per annum. However, one thing that is not taken into account is the way in which the very high salary is whittled down by income tax levels which reach 83 per cent. When this is borne in mind, very often the differential between the highest paid and the lowest paid in a British company is at a ratio that is less than obtains in Soviet Russia for example. For this reason the publication of gross salaries can be very misleading. In the past, there has been opposition to talking about 'take home pay' because it tends *not* to bring into account things like voluntary savings, etc. Maybe if we are to gain greater justice, not only will many other factors need to be taken into account when computing tax, but salaries should perhaps be quoted much more often on a net after-tax basis rather than on the gross figure.

Much thinking is now being done on the whole question of direct taxation, both major political parties making favourable comments on the advantages of indirect taxation. A tax on the difference between income and savings (i.e. a tax on spending) is being actively considered. This in itself makes a job-satisfaction tax more difficult, and to implement it might provoke endless arguments from all kinds of workers who felt that they should be excluded.

One of the most serious by-products of inflation is the erosion of savings. If a government were suddenly to introduce a wealth tax which deprived even the smallest saver of 10, 15 or 20 per cent of his savings each year, the uproar would be so tremendous that the Government would not be able to continue with the extraction of such a proportion of hard-earned wealth. Yet this is precisely what happens when the real value of accumulated savings is attacked by inflation.

Many people would dismiss such an argument, saying that it applies only to the opulent middle-class and therefore is of no real significance. On the contrary, it applies to all sections of the community. Even the person who has an overdraft has possibly a life insurance policy or a pension, and as inflation erodes savings and as the underlying assets in which the insurance fund is invested do not keep pace with inflation, then the amount which is saved for a later period in life is reduced. All we are doing in fact is to

Living in an inflationary world

transfer the debt to a new generation who will in some way or other have to compensate by supporting those who had hoped to support themselves. Many ministers of religion at the beginning of their ministry in the thirties decided that they would take out an assurance policy for £500, which would enable them to purchase a small house on retirement in the seventies. How far £500 would go today to buy a house is only too painfully obvious. It can be calculated that if a minister were to seek to make the same provision in 1977, with the same 40 years' inflation, he would have to think at least in terms of a policy producing £200,000 at the end of 40 years. The premiums for these would be so astronomical as to be quite impossible for him to finance—so he gives up in despair. Such is the effect of inflation on the saving habits of a community. Indeed, there seems to be very little incentive to save at all.

One useful way in which saving has been protected against the inroads of inflation is through the Government index-linked Save As You Earn scheme. For anyone who wants to save regularly and to keep the value of his savings, this is a good scheme. Prior to April 1978 a number of pension funds considered it best to give up the attempt to invest pensions in such a way as to keep up with inflation and accordingly transferred most if not all of their workers' pension provision to the 'Pay As You Go' scheme introduced in the 1975 Social Security Act. That is to say, once again the burden of future pensions is not covered by present savings, which in turn are directed to creating new wealth, not only today but tomorrow. Instead, heavy liabilities are placed unfairly but squarely on the future generation who will be expected out of their contributions at that time to pay the pensions for which money ought to be saved today. The Church has a responsibility to speak up for the future generations who are on present expectations to carry a burden which may be beyond their capacity.

Every Christian has a duty to do his best to ensure that he is not a burden to others in his old age and it is surprising that the Church has not said more about this modern moral problem that the present generation is storing up for the next. We have passed well beyond that phase in our history when we tried to raise as many sons as possible in order that we had a much better chance of reasonable security of living when we were no longer able to work. The effects of inflation have, however, been so severe in the past few years as to jeopardize the whole reality of saving for the future.

7   Credit and two-income morality

Credit morality

Fifty years ago, apart from borrowing money to purchase a house, it was considered improper and imprudent to borrow for the purpose of buying goods. The advent of hire purchase arrangements was regarded by the stolid middle-classes as a dangerous, if not corrupting, innovation. They were not impressed by the economic arguments which were produced to indicate that unemployment could well be brought down by people purchasing well in advance of the time by which sufficient cash could be saved. As the general standard of living of the community has risen, and as the growth of the concept of built-in obsolescence in domestic capital items has increased, so the necessity or the popularity of credit has also increased. This is particularly true in the case of cars, where the cost of a car might represent a sizeable proportion of an annual income and therefore take a very long time to accumulate.

In addition to hire purchase arrangements, personal bank loans and credit cards have become popular. In this country we have not yet reached that point where shopkeepers turn up their noses at cash, but that time might very well arrive, particularly as the disposing of large cash sums becomes more and more a security problem. It is important that the Christian should not be unduly influenced by the remarks of episcopal and other detractors of the system, and it is important to differentiate between the money transfer function of credit cards and the long-term credit function. Except for small items of expenditure, it is often very much more convenient to use a credit card and to pay one cheque or bank transfer slip at the end of the month than it is constantly to walk around with large sums of money or frequently to write out cheques. The danger deriving from credit cards is the great ease with which comparatively large debts can be accumulated. The real rate of interest on some credit cards is comparatively high and masked by the fact that it is calculated on a monthly basis.

The usual argument in favour of credit facilities is that they will stimulate the economy and through growth enable more and more things to be done within the community. The fallacy of this particular argument is that there is a limit to growth, not in mathematical terms but in the ability of the world in which we live to supply all the raw materials that are needed to meet a continuingly expanding economy. A 'dash for growth' as a means of solution to economic problems has been proved doubtful, to say the least, and as John V. Taylor in *Enough is Enough* indicates:

Growth economy is interested in profits, not products; it seeks to reduce labour costs, not to create jobs. As a few of the poorer countries begin to industrialize and knock on the doors of the rich countries, bidding them open their markets, they are met with a cold rebuff in the form of tariffs and quotas. There is something extraordinarily cynical in the argument that the best way to feed the poor is to pile even more upon the rich man's table in the hope that bigger and better crumbs will fall from it.

This is by no means the end of the argument, but it represents a powerful counterblast to the view that growth solves the problems of rich and poor alike.

What is much more reprehensible than taking advantage unwisely of credit facilities, is the attempt to gain credit, sometimes over protracted periods, by not paying bills on time. Individuals have been guilty of this for a long time—for example, never paying rates or electricity accounts until the red notice is received. However, as inflation has produced higher interest rates and as more people have seen the advantages of credit, so the concept of

Credit and two-income morality

enforced borrowing from creditors for as long as they will stand it, has grown. The Inland Revenue now charge interest automatically on bills that are unpaid after a due date, in an attempt to counter this growing habit.

Unfortunately, the big firms are often as guilty as the small ones and in some cases it appears that unduly delaying payment is a deliberate act of policy. There have even been cases of small firms, heavily committed to working for larger ones, that have been driven into bankruptcy because their cash flow has dried up through their accounts not being met on time.

A further unsatisfactory development of the credit economy is that much of the apparatus for the provision of credit is not satisfied with supplying actual demand—it seeks to stimulate it. Possessors of credit cards know that they are subject to subtle—and occasionally not so subtle—pressures from glossy magazines and leaflets to buy; the only requirement is to fill in the form with the credit card number—all the rest will be taken care of! This appears to be unacceptable on ethical grounds for at least two reasons. In the first place it titillates the desire for more material things, probably to a point beyond that which many people can meet out of their income, and therefore inevitably it puts them in a situation where they cannot easily repay their loans. In these instances, whilst not being as bad as getting into the hands of the proverbial rapacious money-lender, an individual is in a position where the very high interest rates tend to regenerate the loan over a long period; the eventual price paid for goods is phenomenally large.

Two-income morality

Wars have a way of changing the habits of a community. One effect of the 1939–45 war was that married women were given a chance to earn their own income. In addition, the development of the ideals of women's liberation has led to the concept of the rightness, particularly where the family is off her hands, of a woman developing a career of her own, or at least of finding a job that is fulfilling in a way that many never found in housework. Originally the intention was to earn a little 'pin money' to supplement the family budget. Later, for many, a dependence upon the income grew as the extra money itself grew. The effect of this trend on life style, of turning luxuries into necessities, has already been mentioned. Other ethical issues are also involved for to some extent there is a new division between rich and poor—i.e. between one and two income families; the latter often more than two times better off than the former, because the second does not have to cover basic provisions like accommodation and heating and lighting.

The tax system, through the dependent wife's allowance, does redress the balance slightly, but unless the incomes are quite large in cash terms the adjustment is relatively small; it is doubtful whether the Treasury has been pressed to consider a greater tax on second incomes. The usual approach is that greater work needs to be rewarded and that any adjustment greater than normal will discourage extra effort. This may be true, but it begs a number of ethical and social questions. For example, are the present incentives such that they lure people away from the proper care of young children? Is the conscientious wife penalized because she puts her children first? In these technological days is it right to assume that the traditional attitude that the man must be the breadwinner irrevocable? Could he not be trained to care for children as adequately as his wife? Are there psychological factors that weigh heavily in the wife's favour in the matter of bringing up children?

This is not to say that the taxman is expected to answer all these questions, but having been answered by society, greater adjustments as between one and two income families might be possible.

8 Church money

The Church today has an ambivalent attitude to money, and this can be seen in all levels of its activity. Locally, on the one hand it stresses the supremacy of 'the spiritual', the importance of mission and preaching, but finds itself often inarticulate when such details are discussed; on the other, it becomes most animated when it comes to talking about jumble sales, bazaars and other devices to raise money, either for work at home or overseas—enthusiasm warms as people grapple with things that they know something about.

The same dichotomy is often found in regional or national meetings, although the emphasis is much more on the theoretical and the abstract. Although some time is spent, perhaps petulantly, discussing money, it is sooner or later asserted that 'we must not spend too much time on money', or 'money must not govern policy'.

What is true in the world at large is true of the Church. Money does not have a life of its own; it is not an entity on its own, to be discussed as an alternative to the 'real' concerns of the Church. Like metres and centimetres, pounds and pence are measurements—in this case usually measuring priorities when resources are limited.

The Church can, of course, fall into those errors which Jesus warns individuals about. It can accumulate too much and be consequently anxious, it can be greedy, prodigal or miserly; it can rely too much on material things, and some would argue it can try to rely too little on them. There are, however, no firm guidelines, no absolutes, and like an individual the Church must be constantly testing its policies and performance against the best available interpretation of New Testament teaching, and by continual reference to the guidance of the Holy Spirit.

The dichotomy between the attitudes of those who concentrate on the 'spiritual' rather than the 'material' can possibly be seen even in glimpses of attitudes expressed by the disciples.

One forms an impression that John is much more 'spiritual' than Peter, and Judas Iscariot clearly allowed his emphasis on the practical and political so to distort his judgement that in the end he was guilty of what is regarded as the worst betrayal in the history of man.

On the whole, the dichotomy was not too prominent during the lifetime of Jesus, no doubt because he was correcting excesses of emphasis on both sides.

In the absence of very detailed accounts it is possible to read too much into the flash of a fragmentary episode, but it might be possible that the handing over of material responsibilities to the seven who were to serve at table (Acts 6:2–4) could be regarded as an early demarcation of attitudes.

The writers in the early Church could be excused for not paying too much attention to material considerations, for they expected the imminent return of Christ. None the less, Paul from time to time does express a sturdy independence, possibly due to his craft of tent making (Acts 18:3; Phillipians 4:11). He did know also what it was like to be on the receiving end of generous hospitality (Phillipians 4:16). He was also concerned to see that poor Christians were well looked after (e.g. 1 Corinthians 16:1).

James was one writer who demonstrated a fundamental sensitivity to material values, but partly because of his theological eccentricities he has been disliked and at times bitterly criticized. To him, faith was meaningless unless it was followed by very practical results. 'Suppose a brother or sister is in rags with not enough food for the day, and one of you says, "Good luck to you, keep yourselves warm, and have plenty to eat", but does nothing to supply their bodily needs, what is the good of that? So with faith; if it does not lead to action, it is itself a lifeless thing' (James 2:16, 17).

James, because of his attitude, was vigorous in his attack on those who exhibited all the failings with regard to riches condemned by Jesus. The strength of his vituperation is reminiscent of Amos, 'Next a word to you who have great possessions. Weep and wail over the miserable fate descending on you. Your riches have rotted; your fine clothes are moth-eaten; your silver and gold have rusted away, and their very rust will be evidence against you and consume your flesh like fire. You have piled up wealth in an age that is near its close. The wages you never paid to the men who mowed your fields are loud against you, and the outcry of the reapers has reached the ears of the Lord of Hosts. You have lived on earth in wanton luxury, fattening yourselves like cattle—and the day for slaughter has come' (James 5:1–5).

These words appear to go further than Jesus did and condemn wealth unconditionally. Apparently James assumes that all wealth is acquired by evil means and he appears even more indignant that the growth of riches occurred in what was regarded as near to the end of the age.

There are considerable dissimilarities between the attitudes shown by James and Paul. Paul appears to write with respect and even affection to the slave-owner Philemon, exhorting in the letter of that name a responsible attitude from one who presumably had great wealth. As happens today, it may be that because Paul had an early background which may have brought him into contact with men of wealth, he learnt to deal with them as individuals on their own merit.

The modern Church has known, and benefited from, many men of wealth, some of recent years, some from centuries ago.

As the Church progressed over the centuries, it became increasingly difficult to disentangle its affairs from the world of money. In the past two centuries, more and more people wished to leave their wealth to the Church, perhaps as an expression of their love for the Lord and his Kingdom, possibly as some cynics have observed, as an insurance for better treatment in the hereafter, to compensate the Lord for a lifetime of dubious practice. Some of the older-established Churches have therefore acquired huge capital sums. Those who are implacable opponents of money within the Church strongly criticize its reliance on money. The legal systems within which the Church and its bequests have to operate, however, make it very difficult for it, even if it so desired, to disentangle itself from its possessions. It is protected by unyielding Charity Law which does not allow it to sell all it has and to give to the poor.

Some of the newer Protestant Churches have very little capital compared to the older denominations. Maybe they are unfortunate, but many within them take the view that, on the contrary, they are blessed, for what they possess is only working capital, building funds, pension funds, etc., and their day-to-day income and expenditure account is not financed by a huge accumulated legacy from the past. This can make people more aware of their own responsibility for maintaining the work of the Church, with the consequence that very often they are able to inject a note of realism into the situation.

This, however, begs one or two important questions, the chief of which is: should the Church have any money at all? Would it not be better for the successors of the disciples to manage without any formal cash arrangements whatsoever? But this in turn is determined by the answer to two further important questions: (a) Should the Church have any premises of its own? and (b) Should the Church have paid clergy?

(a) With financial pressures stemming from a contraction in Church membership and attendance, and from inflationary forces, the local church has found it difficult to maintain its premises and a number of people have ques-

70

Church money

tioned whether, in fact, it is right that it should possess very expensive buildings, particularly since, in the case of worship buildings, they are frequently used only two or three times a week. If they are used more frequently, it is often only by such a small number of people, that the huge cost of heating and lighting them cannot be justified. The alternatives, of course, are for the church to hire a building or a room in which to worship: a room in a hotel or school, a community hall or some other building, has been used by churches, particularly during their infancy and particularly on new estates. Those who have experience of this type of worship-home know only too well how the congregation longs to have its own premises, where it can be master in its own house and organise its own affairs in the most efficient and desirable way, and where there is not the constant problem of overstepping time limits. It may be good for congregations to hear the school caretaker hammer on the door as soon as the hired hour is up, but it is not entirely helpful to a proper sense of worship! It is unreasonable to expect non-churchgoers and even non-Christians to understand the problems associated with conducting services of worship, and it is not easy to transform a school hall or a shop or some other hired room into a place that is conducive to worship.

None the less, the church has to face the cost of its worship centre and although some churches manage to cover total costs by an efficient use of their rooms, by renting them to adult education centres, play groups, etc., the fact remains that the worship centre itself is sometimes too expensive a use of plant within today's financial limitations. The solution is not to abandon a separate building for worship altogether but to reach agreement with other worshipping communities in the same area for the sharing of one building. It should not be beyond the wit of man for three or even four denominations to use one building for services of worship. Admittedly, time schedules have to be carefully worked out, but there are some denominations

71

who traditionally like early services, and some who like them later, and it should be possible to spread them out so that all can be satisfied, even if all have to exercise a little flexibility in their traditional times of worship. Certainly, all would find it very much cheaper, and possibly such an arrangement would enable churchmen to give away far more to those who are in need.

(b) The theological question as to whether or not the Church needs an ordained ministry is not discussed here, but it is obvious that the question as to whether the Church should have a stipendiary clergy has been debated for centuries. No matter what doctrine of the ministry a particular denomination holds, it has become evident that a church which seeks to operate without its own minister (even if shared with one or more other churches) is under a great disadvantage compared with one that *is* so served. It has become a central part of Christian thinking that the flock should have its own shepherd: one who not only rounds up those who are tending to go astray but who also has time to think about the Church as the instrument of Jesus Christ. He can help to design its future activities and has time, for example, to preach a whole series of sermons which will be for the benefit of the people. He becomes one who is, in his own person, a very centre of the life of the church.* Where such a person ceases to exist, church life often withers away, and those churches that have sought to save money by doing away with their minister, tacking their church on to a series of others, have very often found that in the long run they are much worse off than they were, finding that congregations drift off to neighbouring churches that are well-served or, worse still, stay away altogether.

If the Church, then, is to have its own premises to maintain and if it is to have its own clergyman, it is bound to enter into the world of money. Collections or donations, not only to help the poor but to sustain the clergy and to

72

* See *Ordination*, a report to the Methodist Conference, 1974.

Church money

maintain the premises, are inevitable. It is impossible to do this on a day-to-day basis, for money has to be saved up for future expenditure. The prudent church will put away a certain amount each week to deal with necessary repairs and decorations and the payment of the clergy.

Most churches find that a bag or plate passed round on a Sunday does not raise sufficient funds and that a more sophisticated back-up arrangement to ensure the availability of further money is required. There are a number of practices, besides the loose cash collection, for the raising of church money. They are of varying merit.

(1) The most frequently used is an *envelope system* which will enable members to give on a regular basis, so that if they are away, the church can be sure of its regular income. The next time they attend, or through someone who has been to visit them, the envelopes, properly filled with the weekly offering promised, are passed on to the church. These systems are confidential in that often one person, frequently the minister, knows only the names and numbers of the people belonging to the envelope system and another, probably one of the financial stewards, knows only the numbers and the amounts that are contributed week by week. This attempt at secrecy protects the sensitivities of some who believe that it is right that no one should know what they are contributing. Frequently, however, it covers up meanness. Even today it is not unusual to find people placing 10p in the envelope, no doubt believing that they have contributed well and quite oblivious of the fact that what they give scarcely justifies the expense of the envelopes. It is slightly less anonymous, however, than placing loose change, sometimes coppers, in the plate and is probably a step in the right direction. On its own the envelope system does not seem to be adequate and needs some reinforcement by other giving. It also requires constant encouragement of members to update their gifts in the light of individual circumstances and inflation.

(2) *Gift Days*. These are often very successful and relatively painless in terms of effort. What frequently happens is that a congregation is informed by prior publicity what sum is required to balance the church's books and then either the minister sits in the vestry all day to receive gifts, or, alternatively, special envelopes are prepared and circulated, not only to church members but also to the widest church community possible, and gifts are asked for by a particular day. Associated with a Gift Day, church organizations are frequently asked to contribute. In some churches a Gift Day is associated with its anniversary or some other traditional and regular occasion.

(3) *Bazaars and Sales of Work*. These are very popular and many people believe that they are justified by reference to Scripture and in particular by the (perhaps overworked) parable of the talents. Others criticize them strongly on the grounds that they turn the church into a market-place, if not a den of thieves! It is not easy to see who is right. Very large sums are raised by bazaars and many people not closely associated with the church are drawn into the organization and most appear thoroughly to enjoy the exercise. Indeed, if a church moves to some other kind of money-raising system, there are those who bewail the social loss if the bazaar is discontinued. Whilst many people reply that there ought to be other, superior, social and spiritual activities that people can enter into, deploring that so much effort should go into purely commercial schemes rather than into the real work of the church. Others say that this may well be true but people won't do the other sort of work, so that either one faces the loss of the money and possibly their interest, or bazaars are continued.

(4) *Jumble Sales*. These are usually on a much smaller scale, and are less desirable than a bazaar. They are planned only a short time in advance and raise sometimes quite substantial sums. Those involved seldom enjoy them but consider the method a very good way of raising needed

money quickly. The squeamish often find the customers' pushing and scrabbling for secondhand bargains objectionable, and yet they continue to organize them. One of the problems is that if every organization associated with the church (and many that are not) organize jumble sales, there is a grave danger of the church hall becoming known as a secondhand mart rather than the centre of Christian activity. It is probably unreasonable to do away with them altogether, but they should be rationed with some care.

(5) *Lotteries and Bingo*. Many churches turn their back on this form of money raising but some consider it a reasonable method of producing cash for church funds. The objection adduced against the method is that it tends to pander to greed and avarice and that Christians should be willing to help their church willingly and freely and not incidentally through the hope that they will win some substantial prize.

(6) *Stewardship*. 'Stewardship' became popular in the Church in the period following the Second World War. Its methods were derived from those used by certain commercial fund-raising organizations, with adaptations to suit particular needs in individual churches. The great strength of the movement lies in the fact that it causes people to think very carefully about their giving to the church in the context of their general life-style. Ostensibly, money is not the only objective; indeed, much of the stewardship director's time is devoted to persuading people that the giving of time and talents is at least as important as money.

This emphasis helps to ensure that the whole campaign does not degenerate into a purely money-raising jamboree, and most churches that have conducted such campaigns maintain that they have been spiritually stimulated in a way that none could remember happening before. Great spiritual benefits are claimed to have accrued, including new members added to the roll.

In a big church the actual campaign could last several weeks, with months of preparation preceding the

75

inauguration at a special church dinner, when the principles are explained by carefully rehearsed speakers. Thereafter, all those attending the dinner are visited by teams of trained visitors who elicit pledges of time, talents and money. These are not entirely secret, which is disliked by some church members.

The result of the campaign are carefully assessed and usually show that a large number of people are willing to perform certain duties in the church, or have indicated that they will ferry old folks to services, cut their lawns, and perform other useful social activities. Finance, which is the criterion, one suspects, by which many judge the success of the campaign, usually involves at least a doubling and sometimes a trebling of the Sunday's collection. A large harvest of covenanted subscriptions also follows.

So great is the apparent success of the campaigns that many feel it is the solution to all our problems and some suggestions have been made that before central grants are offered, churches are to be required to have campaigns. Thus, in the absence of any serious rival, stewardship campaigns are still regarded as the best way of galvanizing the church into activity and restoring its financial equilibrium. There are, however, a number of question marks over the whole idea which are long overdue for careful examination.

In the first place, there is a strong element of artificiality involved in a campaign. Whilst there is no doubt that the church dinner is a jolly social occasion, having some positive good in its bringing virtually the whole church community together, it appears curiously out of place if it is admitted that it is the only method known—and especially in the early days, a very expensive one at that—of inaugurating a successful campaign. On the cynical (but undoubtedly true) assumption that few will resist a free dinner, the whole design of the campaign is based. The dinner must be held where the whole community can gather, and if the church hall is not big enough, then a larger one must be hired. Do-it-yourself dinners were not originally acceptable, because a proportion of chief workers were siphoned off at the critical moment of the campaign. This rule has been relaxed in most campaigns and less elaborate meals have proved acceptable, and just as effective.

In one sense, of course, there can be nothing wrong in giving people a free meal, but to base an important strategy in the church's work on an appeal to the baser instincts of people appears theologically suspect unless it is contended that to 'set a sprat to catch a mackerel' is a good illustration of Christians being wiser than serpents!

As far as one is aware no one has undertaken a careful investigation into the long-term results of stewardship campaigns. Such an enquiry may well demonstrate that the momentum of such campaigns is quick to retard. A repeat campaign appears necessary almost every year or two thereafter; otherwise, with the movement of population, the proportion of membership involved quickly decreases and the amounts which continue to be given do not reflect the inroads of inflation on the value of the currency. This repeat campaign is an ongoing expense of some substance and cannot be overlooked when assessing the net benefit of the campaign.

The momentum of time and talents tends to die quicker than that of money. In the first flush of enthusiasm people will promise to do all kinds of things which quickly get crowded out when faced with the other demands on their energies. Another problem appears to be that in many instances the organization for the use of time and talents is not as efficient as that for finance and many of the offers are not taken up. This may be because the organizers are sometimes surprised by the volume of offers, and by the time they are able to make some suggestion for the use of the proffered time and talent, the volunteer has other ideas. Later campaigns have reduced suggested opportunities for the exercise of talents in favour of a deeper, but perhaps more vague call for commitment certainly the general trend of Stewardship campaigns has become more evangelical.

One of the major effects, and perhaps the most serious, is that no matter how much income does increase, it rarely increases enough to budget adequately for contingencies. Many are the churches that previously, when faced with unexpected expenses such as a burst boiler, would shrug their shoulders and call for a special gift day or bazaar which would resolve the problem. After a stewardship campaign this is no longer permissible, and the church is faced either with reneging on its promise to ask for nothing further than the member's all-in pledge, or to cut back on some other item for which it has budgeted. The most likely sufferer is charitable giving, such as overseas missions (which reports a decline of income from churches espousing stewardship) or important maintenance which results in facing greater problems later. This situation becomes more acute as the years from the initial campaign pass. More recent campaigns have ceased emphasizing 'all-in-giving' to make it easier to have emergency special efforts. This does however appear to undermine a central theme of stewardship.

On closer examination, the distinction between time, talents and money appears less certain. How can one use talents without expending time? For most people money represents the stored rewards of the use of past talents. Some members have monotonous jobs or skills which cannot be translated into cash; some have jobs which require them to work long hours. If the contribution from the latter has a higher cash content than that of the former, is it any the less welcome or to be disregarded? The sale of work is occasionally despised because it is 'commercial', and whilst it must be admitted the last thing we want the church to become is a trading organization, there appears to be nothing theologically wrong with people changing their talents of knitting, for example, into garments which are subsequently sold for charitable purposes. Yet this use of talents is condemned by those who think the only approach is through the principle of stewardship.

One of the great benefits of the stewardship campaign is that it does concentrate the mind firmly on the whole question of giving to God. Such campaigns have ruthlessly exposed the arbitrary and often pitiful nature of 'loose change' giving. To return to the vagaries of the previous system would be a seriously regressive step. Any replacement of the stewardship concept must move forward. One thing stewardship has done is to emphasize the spiritual reaction of a warm response of gratitude for what God has done for us. Much of our budgeting approach appears to stem from an idea that we should never give more than is absolutely necessary—ensuring, say some, that we always have rather less than we need!

7. *Tithing.* What is needed today is not a new theology of money, but a fresh interpretation of old theology in today's terms, and an effective but simple presentation of it to the people. The most successful system of giving ever invented was the tithe. Going back to Moses, and perhaps even earlier, it represents a very simple system of giving to God (even if through the priests) and setting aside money for the poor.

Today, tithing is practised by only a tiny minority of the Church. It requires a degree of devotion that the majority of church members would find disagreeable, for it involves on average an increase of giving of up to eight times. Today many consider it an unfair system in that the higher the income earned, the higher the rate of tax. In the highest tax bracket of all, when the unearned income levy is deducted, the Chancellor of the Exchequer does not leave 10 per cent of that part of a persons' income. Today, through taxation and social security payments, most people make a substantial donation towards the upkeep of the poor (although up to now we have not done all that well in relation to the poor of other lands except in the case of the comparatively small numbers we have admitted into this country). One clear advantage of the tithe is that it automatically adjusts giving to match increased income.

A modern fair system of giving should be based on net spendable income or 'take home pay'. It would also need to acknowledge that some people have much higher expenses than others—if they have, say, teenage children.

Some people would like a very clear statement of what would be a reasonable amount to give to the church and other charitable funds. Such a table would not be difficult to produce, but the more sophisticated it becomes the more it would resemble a system of taxation; indeed, it could be argued that a system of giving based on the income tax an individual paid is the fairest system of all! It would also be the most unpopular and would not take into account a spontaneous warmth which is an essential ingredient in every true gift to God.

Possibly some system of a 'mini tithe' might be considered. It could be based on take-home pay, and in view of the way taxation, etc., takes care of much of the poor of our own country, it might be argued that half a tithe (5 per cent) could be the norm. Some allowance would have to be made for individual circumstances, but this allowance should be the decision of the member and no one else, with generosity being measured by how much one deducted from the 'mini tithe' rather than how much extra one put in the plate.

True giving stems from a true faith; the more we become identified with God the more we regard what we have as his, and the less difficult it is to prise us away from it! Further, this responsible approach to money management leads to a reciprocal benefit. The whole of one's life is transformed, because a new value is given to Christian faith; it becomes something that is embedded in the hard cement of reality and not woven like a spider's web in the breeze of ephemeral dreams.

8 *Covenanted giving* Whilst not a method of giving, the seven year deed of covenant is a very fruitful source of

church income. The Methodist scheme is the largest in the country, and in 1978 resulted in over £1m in income tax being refunded.

Any member paying tax can covenant identifiable gifts to the church, provided he is willing to continue such payments for a period of seven years. Gifts to the church through the envelope system or direct subscriptions to church organizations can be included in such covenants.

The Methodist scheme involves covenanting through a central organization which for a small charge records the covenant and reclaims the tax. Any subsequent transfer of membership to another Methodist church is allowable, and the subscriber is entitled to nominate which Methodist charity or charities, including his local church, he wishes to benefit from the tax recovered.

Some criticize the system on the grounds that it is a tax dodge or involves requiring the rest of the community to pay for one's pet charity. Successive Chancellors of the Exchequer have, however, explicitly commended covenanting to charities as a way in which the State can support charitable work.

Many charities believe that the system is preferable to the 'tax-deductible' system which exists in some other countries. Although the latter has the advantage from the donor's point of view that he needs to consider only one year's giving at a time, from the charities' point of view it has two large disadvantages. One is that it loses the guaranteed seven years' income. The other is that the tax-deductible system involves the subscriber himself saving the tax on his gift, whereas when under the covenant scheme £1 is subscribed from taxed income, the charity receives back all the tax on the gift as it was before tax was levied, perhaps adding half as much again to the money given. In America it has been calculated that charities actually receive only half what tax payers have said they have given, whereas under the covenanting, there is very little opportunity to abuse the system.

As with any other kind of giving, the covenantor needs to update his giving regularly with a series of new deeds, or a Superceding Deed. The latter is a completely new deed, capable of exceeding six years, for a sum larger than the one it replaces.

9 Political attitudes to money

At the beginning of the industrial era the role of government was extremely limited, and even the introduction of 6d in the pound income tax was regarded as an intolerable intrusion into private liberty. Gradually, however, the power of government has increased over the years until many today believe that it plays too prominent a part in the financial management of a country. This is not universally accepted by economists, some of whom maintain that, although a government can, as it were, put suitable 'trims' on the steering, it cannot easily engineer a large change of course. Certainly governments, by their fiscal policies, can take money out of the hands of the population or, by reducing income tax or other taxes, can stimulate the economy and seek to improve an ailing economic situation.

All kinds of political measures are used today and some maintain that the government operates so much and in times of stress so frequently with changes of direction and stop-go policies, that its frenzied action is self-defeating because it creates uncertainty and unwillingness to plan far in advance for fear that external forces under government control will stop plans or render them unprofitable.

However, although possibly in times of crisis the Government might tend to over-react in order to seek to right a serious situation it is obviously quite impossible for a Government today to allow the *laissez-faire* policies of the entrepreneurial days to exist in modern society. Quite apart from the necessity of financing the Welfare State in its various facets, including support for the poor and underprivileged, the sick and the old, many of the excesses of the earlier free enterprise activities have had to be curtailed by law. For example, the law against monopoly and cartel activities now prevents the possibility of a few business men acquiring much of the wealth of the country by holding the population to ransom.

Nowadays, Government control of industry is not only through fiscal action but is comprehensive enough to determine the number of washbasins, lavatories, rest rooms, etc., that are on business and office premises and to set minimum temperatures, safety and fire regulations, and strict control of staff appointments, employment and dismissals. The number of differing regulations now becomes to many businesses, especially small ones, almost oppressive. Any Government that is seeking the welfare of the people at large by introducing new regulations has, of course, to weigh the cost to the community of extra resources of man-power and money needed to maintain and supervise any further regulations which are introduced. In 1976 the activities of the Government in seeking to restore confidence in an ailing pound were vigorous. A useful and powerful agreement over a two-year period from 1975/77 (continuing more modestly in 1978) between the Government and the TUC has certainly enabled what appeared to be an almost unstoppable inflationary spiral to be halted at least temporarily, and the rate of inflation to be reduced from near 30 per cent to single figures. However, despite this remarkable performance, the Government had to contend with the awakening fears and uncertainties of foreigners, who at long last, indeed surprisingly late in the day, had worries about the future of the pound. Amongst the economies of the West, the unemployment rate in Great Britain was low, although most unions and many business men would regard the figure of 1½ million as being intolerably high. The price, however, of maintaining in the face of an international slump the comparatively low level of unemployment, partly through high Government expenditure, has been a higher rate of inflation than elsewhere and a balance of payments deficit, which despite all efforts, appeared for a time impossible to reduce to manageable proportions. Fortunately, North Sea oil seems to have come to the rescue of the country, by improving the balance of payments position.

Those who believe in a directly interventionist God can be forgiven for believing that he has singularly favoured this nation. Not only have we avoided the devastations of earthquake, hurricane and vast floods, but we have been richly endowed with massive natural resources. For example, our coal, together with an inventiveness above average, ensured that we led the way in the Industrial Revolution and in the chase for national wealth. We were also endowed with a temperament and insularity which avoided the excesses of continental revolution and therefore enabled governments to steer the country with minimum interference to a large expansion of the Gross National Product.

Out of the new-found wealth successive governments were able to introduce a series of social measures that righted one by one all the major ills of society. Some ensured that production increased still further—at least for a time. Universal education has produced a comparatively literate workforce that at all levels has been able to grasp the intricacies of production needs and initially to push the frontiers of method to new limits, far more quickly than our competitors. The almost incidental acquisition of an empire gave useful markets beyond our own and increased the availability of cheap natural resources, and labour—a matter of ethical consideration in its own right.

The development by governments of free medical services has ensured the emergence of a comparatively healthy work force, free from debilitating illnesses which in epidemics and certain occupational diseases strike at the roots of good industrial order.

From the Christian point of view the progress towards social equality and amelioration made by successive governments is all to the good. Inevitably, it must appear as progress of some substance towards Christian ideals.

None the less, it is curious that within this pioneering social development there are what some see as seeds of weakness, if not of destruction of the whole social system, through the undermining of a willingness or even ability to work. In retrospect, it is clear that out of the undoubted evils of insecurity, fear and adversity there developed a toughness born of desperation. From the toughness came the will which in turn matched the necessity to work unbelievably hard. Unless the old-time employer had more than a full day's work out of his employees, he would find others to take their place. Similarly, if they showed the slightest propensity to sickness over any period, they were often fired. Out of this insensitivity and social evil there emerged a strong economy. We are now enjoying the riches which are the direct or indirect result of this ruthless drive.

No Christian could conceivably expect people to work so hard as they were forced to a century ago. However, the fact is that production has tailed off in terms of output per man-hour far more than it has with our competitors in the Western world. Possibly some of the trouble is attributable to poor capital investment (itself caused possibly by too much Government intervention), some perhaps to indifferent management. A large part, however, may well be due to a social security system that so cushions difficulty and disaster, that it renders the individual often unwilling to work hard; if he goes on strike for a few weeks his family is helped substantially by social security benefits and he is covered, at least initially, by income tax refunds. It is clearly discernible that the 'strike season' (October–March) coincides with the greatest tax refunds available. Many would argue, however, that this need not be the only choice. Japan, for example, has approached the whole problem differently. In the giant industrial firms like Toyota, a very different attitude to the workforce has been engendered. We would not like it in this country because of its paternalism but it overcomes the great problem of social security and worker-care in such a way that production per employee is vastly higher than here. It is perhaps sad that it has to be left to a non-Christian country to demonstrate that a genuine care for workers from cradle to grave can, and perhaps should, be operated in the context of life-time employment in a firm and happy industrial relationships. Mass sackings, lay-offs, strikes and walk-outs are virtually unknown. Perhaps the Japanese temperament has something to do with it, and possibly their late arrival on the industrial scene. However, unless we are able to solve our labour problems better we shall get poorer and poorer.

One of the major problems on the British scene is the great Trade Union movement which has rapidly gained in strength. Successive governments have had good cause to fear union power, and of recent years, when they have fought them they have lost. (cf. Barbara Castle and *In place of strife*, Edward Heath and the miners, and the Industrial Relations Act). The power of the unions has also supported the introduction of such a plethora of regulations regarding conditions of service and dismissal that some employers consider that the dice is loaded so heavily against them that they can never hope to be truly profitable and competitive with overseas firms. Many, however, would strenuously deny this assertion, whether or not there are ethical problems associated with union power is dealt with later, but a real problem emerges for the Christian from social advance. Not only has the overall production of wealth reduced, making it more difficult to give to the poorer nations but it has been incurred in an attempt to apply Christian principles and achieve Christian aims. It seems not so much that the original aims were wrong—indeed, if society is to seek to express the compassion of Christ, they are vital—but that much more work needs to be done on the ways of achieving them and of minimizing any disadvantages that may accrue to them.

Furthermore the earlier Genesis idea of work being a punishment appears here to have a suspicion of support.

Modern society tends to regard most work as being far less than a state of bliss. If work is not the result of punishment, at least it is regarded by many as 'hard labour'! Not only has much human progress arisen through an instinctive recoil from hard work—for example, the progression in the cutting of wood by flint axes, to iron-age axes, hand saws, and early mechanical saws and then to the latest bandsaws which require virtually no effort at all to operate—but the gradual reduction of hard work has a tendency to increase a reluctance, leading eventually to an inability, to engage in it at all. Hard physical work is not the only type affected—it appears that in twenty years' time there will hardly be a soul in the country that can multiply five by five without reaching for a calculator. It is not suggested that there is anything intrinsically wrong with a trend away from 'hard grind'—only that in progress away from physical and mental work there are inherent dangers. Better mechanical apparatus may result in progress for the community; on the other hand the work saving, or potential work saving, even if as a result of a humanitarian desire to make work more tolerable, could result in unemployment accompanied sometimes by an increasing lack of desire to work. This is, of course, not to say that all those sick or unemployed are losing the desire to work. More often than not the contrary is true, and it is impossible to measure, for example, the degradation and the spiritually debilitating effects of a protracted period of knowing that one is not wanted and feeling useless. The effects of the trend are often more clearly seen in those who are working and fear nothing and care for nothing, including production and unemployment.

The problem for the Christian in all this is the blunt fact that the more the community helps people, sometimes the less they are willing to help themselves. If the progress towards humanitarianism proceeds in such a way that only those who really enjoy their work feel a need to work, the gain to society is dubious. The Christian cannot stop caring for the needy, but against all the instincts of compassion

Political attitudes to money

there appears to be the need carefully to weigh the results of each course of action.

In our country, great emphasis has rightly been laid on the defects of our economic system, particularly as they have affected people. Christians can only applaud attempts to right the wrongs of the system. Many have gone much further and asserted that the whole system is fundamentally evil and must be completely changed. But Christians cannot be said to have any valid approach to money or wealth until they are clear about the morality of holding it and the methods of producing it. We therefore turn to an assessment of these questions.

As soon as a Stone Age man had put an edge on a flint to make a tool, or stripped an animal of a skin to make rudimentary clothes, he could be said to have produced wealth. Indeed, even at this primitive level all the modern problems of wealth have detectable antecedents; e.g. wealth means power for the man with an axe and possibly subjugation for the man without; the man with clothes has to decide how much he must share with the one still naked, particularly in times of extreme cold. In this sense of the word at least, man could not exist, particularly in the colder climates, without wealth and to stay alive required the production of wealth.

There is little evidence in the New Testament that workers believed the world of reality is to be shunned in favour of the 'spiritual world'. Such concepts, although to be found in early Christian heresies, are mainly the work of later workers and thinkers. Paul, although at times dominated by important theological considerations, has some powerful things to say regarding the necessity of supporting oneself with earned wealth: 'We were no idlers among you; we did not accept board and lodging from anyone without paying for it; we toiled and drudged, we worked for a living night and day, rather than be a burden to any of you. . . .For even during our stay with you we laid down the rule: the man who will not work shall not eat (2 Thess. 3:7–10).

Jesus himself did not appear to regard the acquisition of wealth as evil in itself. It is obviously dangerous to draw too many conclusions from the parables. He even appears to regard wealth and the acquisition of wealth as something which could be used to win friendship in this life and

The possession of wealth

commendation in the life hereafter. (Luke 16:9 'So that when money is a thing of the past, you may be received into an eternal home'). This may be evidence of the view of Jesus that the end of the world was imminent, as Schweitzer and others have suggested, or it may be an indication that the material things of this world are to be treated with transitional respect in so far as that when the end of life comes, the only value they have is that they have helped us to come to terms with the proper approach to the spiritual world.

Whilst Jesus exhorts men to exert themselves to produce wealth, which will enable them to live in an abundant world, equally and frequently he warns them of the dangers of allowing these activities to become an obsession to the point at which they are over-balanced in their attitudes. 'Beware! Be on your guard against greed of every kind, for even when a man has more than enough, his wealth does not give him life' (Luke 12:15). This is followed by the forbidding tale of the farmer who was doing so well that he needed new store-houses, and so he pulled down the old ones, only to find that life itself had reached an end. 'You fool, this very night you must surrender your life; you have made your money—who will get it now?' That is how it is with the man who amasses wealth for himself and remains a pauper in the sight of God. The lyrical passage that follows (Luke 12.22ff), perhaps echoing the words of the Sermon on the Mount (Matthew 6:25ff), is not an exhortation to dispense with all forms of planning and arrangement. It is an exhortation against anxiety and fretful worry. The word *merimnai* means anxiety or care; or as Vincent Taylor in his commentary (Mark 4:18), says: '*by hai merimnai tou aionos* is meant worldly care, anxiety arising out of the times, worry.' The sort of anxiety that comes from one who has wealth which induces within him such fears of it being stolen, or destroyed, or lost, that his mind is for ever with it. 'For where your treasure is, there will your heart be also' (Matthew 6:21).

This neurotic looking backward, or intense consideration for the wealth which he had left behind, led Jesus to
advise the young man who sought to enter the Kingdom of
Heaven, to sell his possessions and give to the poor and he
would have riches in heaven, then to follow him (Matthew
19:22). The man is reported to have gone away with a
heavy heart, because he was of great wealth. This is followed by the picturesque and sad comment from Jesus: 'It
is easier for a camel to pass through the eye of a needle,
than for a rich man to enter the Kingdom of God.' What is
usually forgotten is that the episode is concluded by the
disciples wondering who on earth could be saved, and Jesus
saying: 'For men, this is impossible; but everything is possible for God' (Matthew 19:26). Many interpretations of
this incident have been made by preachers and writers—some seeking to prove that all wealth is bad; some
seeking to make it easier for rich people to take heart.

This cautionary attitude towards wealth is entirely in line
with the teaching that Jesus gives elsewhere, for a man who
was looking backwards all the time would not be fit for the
vigorous mental and spiritual exercise that was in store for
a true follower. One recognizes that the words are spoken
in the context of a period when it was very difficult to store
wealth, which might well be in the form of sheep or goats;
or if it were in the form of valuable objects, would need the
personal supervision of the owner himself. This could be a
very considerable strain, for unless the man was physically
present all the time, he could not be sure that his associates
or servants would not make off with the valuable possessions that he had. Once again, we have not so much a
teaching against wealth, but rather a pointer to the
psychological and spiritual dangers that attend those who
have many possessions. Nonetheless we ignore the warnings of Jesus at our peril and recognize that the more we
possess the greater the struggle to pass through the eye of a
needle. Clearly also, the texts cannot be taken as a guide to
a proper approach for the modern Christian. It is quite

The possession of wealth

impossible to extract advice that is tended to one who is in an entirely unsophisticated economic system, and place it in modern conditions. The effect of a vast number of people piously selling all that they have to give to the poor, would only add astronomically to the number of poor that had to be supported by the rest of the community. Instead of accepting a degree of responsibility for oneself, one is placing that responsibility on others, and the more people who do it, the fewer there are to accept the load, until the time comes, of course, when it is entirely impossible to bear. This kind of thinking, this abdication of personal responsibility, does not appear to be in line with the teaching that Jesus made throughout the Gospels.

Where human beings are at work and given a multitude of differing talents, the amount of wealth that each accumulates will be varied. Indeed, the management of one's resources also affects the wealth that is accumulated, for even if you are very good at filling up the bucket, if you are equally good at spilling it, it never becomes very full.

This is one of the problems that is seldom dealt with by those who seek an entirely egalitarian society in the name of Jesus Christ. However, it is well within the Christian context to seek, through humanitarian grounds, to minimize the differences between rich and poor. This is done partly by encouraging the poor to help themselves and to earn more and then to manage what they have more adequately, but partly it may be accomplished by the rich who, of their own free will and from a basis of love, donate to those who are in need. The early Christians certainly were frequently engaged in making collections for the poor. Paul himself was an organizer (cf. 1 Corinthians 16:1).

In the early days of the Industrial Revolution and in the great upsurge of capitalist expansion in this country, any alternative to the generally accepted system of producing wealth was left to a minute minority to commend, and they were dismissed as dangerous revolutionaries. Although there were early manifestations of the many disadvantages of the market economy the basic assumption of the community in general appeared to be that it had to be adjusted rather than completely changed. Things then were very much as the American scene is now, with virtually no admitted alternative to the capitalist system. In that country, in the aftermath of the witchhunt of McCarthy (apart from aberrations within a few college campuses) Communism is still thought of by most as tantamount to anti-Americanism.

Whether it was the British tradition of muddling through, or another attempt to find our way gradually to new ideas, it is difficult to say, but thinking regarding State planned economy began to emerge, not so much initially as a practical alternative to the capitalist system, but as a Utopian goal towards which those who thought themselves oppressed could strive. Tawney and those who were with him in the Christian Socialist movement had a powerful influence on this thinking.

Within the Socialist movement there were however, as there are today, distinct traditions: those which are scarcely indistinguishable from Communism and those which tend to a more European Social Democratic concept. Unfortunately the term 'socialist' is used in a number of different ways by different people; in the pages that follow, unless otherwise stated 'Communism' is used very broadly to refer to the extreme Left. The British brand of socialism is largely despised by international Communism, although in its extreme form it is difficult to distinguish socialism from Communism.

When in Government Socialism moves with extreme caution and appears content with a mixed economy of State and private enterprise, sometimes handing back to a Conservative government with only a few changes, not all of which appear unacceptable to the other party. Perhaps because there was this less radical alternative the Communist party of Great Britain has seldom been viewed with much popularity and at the time of some of the East-European satellite uprisings and their inevitable crushing by the Soviet military power, it lost many members. The cautious approach by the British Labour Party to a complete State planned economy perhaps suits our particular dislike of extremes. It enables those who so desire, to praise the State planned economy without the painful changes which the implementation of such a system would require. None the less, over the past few years the Left of the Labour Party has become stronger at national as well as constituency level and the strains have increased in the coalition to such an extent that a complete rift would never be surprising. A coalition of the centre parties would inevitably involve a re-alignment of the Left, and the hidden 'strength' of the more radical socialists would be revealed for the first time. However, at present poll samples all appear to indicate that the British are as a whole politically in the middle of the road.

The established Church has in the past been fairly closely associated with the Conservative Party and therefore has been thought to want the market economy system virtually unchanged. There have been notable exceptions. Archbishop William Temple, and many sensitive people such as the then Prince of Wales, later Edward VIII, and Dick Shepherd and others, felt that some revision of economic policies was essential.

The concept of the social gospel which followed the First World War grew in favour amongst Christians. It was believed that the only way to a man's soul was through his stomach, or putting it another way, one could not dare preach to him the love of God until one had demonstrated in a practical way that this required one to feed and clothe him beforehand. Incidentally, the effectiveness of this particular brand of preaching was later proved to be most inadequate. As the standard of living rose, the people who once queued up to attend soup kitchens and receive clothing from the missions showed that in their more affluent period they no longer had any need for such attentions and absented themselves conspicuously from the scene of their degradation.

The social gospel, interpreted later as a new and fiery brand of Christian socialism by Donald Soper and others, proclaimed fiercely that if one was not a socialist it was very difficult, if not impossible, to be a Christian. The capitalist system was doomed and was iniquitous because fundamentally it was based on self-interest; God could not operate, and his Kingdom could not be built on such base foundations. Such sentiments were all the more emphasized by the apparent iniquity of the system. Unemployment, which was running high at that time, condemned men to the scrap heap, to the degradation of being unwanted and a burden upon the rest of society.

Theologically, it was considered very difficult, if not impossible, to reconcile the teaching of a God who, through Jesus Christ, condemned greed and exhorted men and women to behave as brothers and sisters and to care for one another by self-sacrifice and with love, to a political philosophy which required the greatest profit to be made, often in the quickest time and without regard to social consequences.

Those who sought to defend the capitalist system, though attacked frequently, pointed to good Christian men and women who had worked within it and who, having

Politics and the production of wealth

succeeded, had demonstrated a degree of mercy and generosity with the wealth they had acquired. Perhaps also they had shown understanding and caring for those whom they employed during the process of making the profit. It was a defensive approach and very little effort was made at any deep level to reconcile the philosophy with the gospels. Of course, at a rather limited level they pointed to the parable of the talents and the exhortation to make the most of them, but faced with the fiery red heat of Christian socialism the only effective retort that they could make was to turn away disdainfully and say that politics should not be mixed up with religion. There was a very fervent dislike amongst most church people of all denominations for any introduction of politics into the Sunday service, so that the defence, although fundamentally defective, proved surprisingly successful.

Today, people are still questioning the correctness of the role of the market economy, because it does not appeal to idealists and it still seems to have many basic flaws. These are emphasized in our own country at the present time when our economic situation has become worse. Whilst other European countries show no sign of a strong leftward movement, our own country is hovering, uncertain which way to turn. The capitalist scene has been blamed for the weakness of the country, although many outside economists have blamed the reckless spending of various governments. Scandals of various kinds have swept across the City of London, such as led a past Conservative Prime Minister to describe one as representing 'the unacceptable face of capitalism'. Given the apparent unease of Christians (theologically at any rate) when faced with the rigours of the capitalist system, can any attempt to mend, patch or reorganize the system ever prove to be satisfactory? Those who answer in the negative are faced with the uncomfortable choice of the State owned and planned system. Although many of its economic tenets, and indeed the philosophical ones also, have some things in common with

97

Christianity, the basic point of disagreement is over the value placed on the individual. Whereas in Communism, the extreme form of socialism, the classless society is the supreme aim for which all else must be sacrificed, in Christianity care of the individual is of greatest importance. 'To each according to his need and from each according to his ability' appears to be a reasonable line for any Christian to take. The problem has always been in the implementation of such a concept and making it a viable State proposition.

Various systems have been tried within the Communist orbit, but one fatal flaw has always been apparent. You might in theory call men comrades, think that it was entirely wrong for anyone to make a profit and that for a State to own all things was the most important thing to aim at—in practice you had to cope with ordinary people who were unchanged and self-centred and desirous of achieving the best they could for themselves and their families.

The Communist system has never been conspicuously successful economically. For example, in the past sixty years, that is since the Revolution, Russia's wheat production has not increased at all, but in the same period American production of wheat has trebled. This, of course, is not a conclusive proof of the efficiency of one system and the inefficiency of the other; all the difficulties involved in seeking to introduce modern methods amongst peasant farmers were experienced very sharply by the Soviets. However, it illustrates the difficulty of implementing what at first sight seems a noble philosophy to unredeemed human nature. There is ample evidence that when a bureaucrat plans, he does so with nothing like the sensitivity engendered in the entrepreneur who is liable to lose everything if he makes a mistake. A recent visitor to Russia discovered a product being made with nuts and bolts instead of a much cheaper welding process, simply because a bureaucrat somewhere had ordered millions of nuts and bolts which could only be used up in this way. Examining the growth factors of both America and Russia in the past fifty years, the enormous efficiency, if not ruthlessness of the American system appears quite clearly to be more powerful in terms of its productive capacity than the Communist system.

Does that mean it is any better? Certainly not, but as the Communist system has never been politically successful unless it has also been accompanied by a police state system that requires all the objectionable paraphernalia which is associated with totalitarian government, it is difficult to see that idealistically this is any improvement on capitalism from the Christian point of view.

It is true that much of our experience of Communism is derived from Russia and Eastern European states. A new type, it is sometimes argued, is being developed in some developing countries of Africa and Asia. Whether experience will show it varying from what we now see, is difficult to say.

Many Christians have desperately been turning away from both Communism and capitalism in the search for an alternative in the hope that somehow or other something new may be discovered. Certainly there is universal dissatisfaction with the international (transnational) companies, and the very large and mainly insensitive state corporations which appear to be little different, except that on the whole they lose more money than the former.

At the close of the war, with the nationalization of the mines, any who were associated with the mining communities knew how a great ripple of excitement was felt by many of the old political performers believing that the 'millenium' had come, their dream of decades had been achieved and that now the miners would own mines and all would be well. Thirty years later, the dream has been forgotten and the relationship between the State and the miners does not appear to be so conspicuously different from the earlier period with the mine owners, except that the erstwhile owners were more clearly identified, and with them both agreements and hostility were possible on a personal level and were therefore simpler. Now in frustration and dissatisfaction, the miner feels that he must sometimes hold the country up to ransom in order to ensure that he is not a loser in the battle for the highest wages. The socialist dream has been lost in the private enterprise of the National Union of Mineworkers making every attempt to improve the lifestyle and standards of its members. Similarly the year 1977, when Government thoughts were moving towards a third in a series of pay policies, most of the big union leaders indicated a desire for 'a return to free collective bargaining'. What this meant, other than a private enterprise system, it is difficult to see. Few appeared to perceive the inconsistency of, embracing socialist philosophies most powerfully and sincerely, yet advocating a system which benefited the strong rather than the weak.

It is important to note that for a Communist system particularly, to operate successfully, one minimum precondition appears absolutely essential and that is that those within it are totally Christian. That is to say, that their motivation has been so completely changed that they regard God as the ruler and will subject all their own desires and inclinations to his judgement and his guidance and are prepared quite happily to see others achieve where they do not. In a pluralist society it appears unlikely that this pre-condition will ever be met.

Whilst not Christian at all, the Red Guard revolution in China is the nearest that the Communist world has ever seen to a religious revival, and although to our Western eyes the sight of Red Guards chanting slogans, holding little red books encapsulating the thoughts of Mao, seems to us to be quite fatuous, there is no doubt that the fervour that was generated throughout that entire vast country was very considerable. Remarkable achievements were made simply because in the interests of the community and in the love and loyalty to Chairman Mao they were prepared to sacrifice virtually everything. This fiery religious spirit was never seen in the same way in the Soviet Union. Indeed, the revolutionary zeal was much more pedestrian and degenerated all the quicker, so much so that the concept of the profit motive has had to be introduced into Russian production in order to ensure that more efficient systems can be introduced and less efficient ones abolished.

All this has of course separated the Chinese and Russian Communists, the former regarding the latter as revisionists and traitors to the Communist cause. For those who live long enough it will be interesting to see a similar 'degenerative' process begin in China, for the evidence is that it is impossible to sustain the white-hot religious heat of a revolutionary movement for more than a decade or so. In the last few years changes have been made which cause mary to believe that extreme idealism in China has given way to pragmatic considerations.

The early Christians sought to achieve a Communist system where everything was pooled. There were many who espoused it with joy, some with less than enthusiasm, such as Ananias who sought to come in and yet still retain his own private possessions. The whole experiment was an abysmal failure and the Church rapidly turned its back on it, leaving it as an aberration best forgotten. If the system is not successful when run by and for committed Christians, so soon after the resurrection of their Lord, does it stand much chance of success in any circumstances?

Is a capitalist system as bad as it is sometimes made out to be? Undoubtedly it is often worse. The question is, if there is no other workable alternative to Communism, can the market economy system in its present curtailed form ever be acceptable to the Christian? It is, then, necessary for us to look very carefully at the previous Christian criticisms of the market economy and see if these actually hold water, and if they do to decide whether proper changes can be made. As has been noted in previous paragraphs, human nature has always to be taken into account. It is no good having any political or economic philosophy that takes no notice of instinctive human reactions.

From the beginning of time, the human being, to survive, had to be alert to his own interests and, if necessary, to defend himself. It cannot be denied that God has given him this inbuilt instinct. If man is not hungry he does not eat, and if he does not eat he dies. Fortunately, we do not live in a part of the world where one has to fight for one's food. In the earliest primitive conditions this was essential and only the strongest survived. This instinct of self preservation, however, remains an ineradicable part of human nature. We might complain all we can about how wrong it is that man should feel in this way and we might seek by all the means at our disposal and call upon Almighty God to assist us in order to change man, but then it is impossible for him to cut out entirely the instinctive consideration of his own personal position relating to any given circumstance at any given time. The more mature or perfect a Christian the man is, the more he might, having looked at the situation, opt for the nobler solution, but this is the most that can happen and the world in which we live is not mainly comprised of people of this spiritual calibre or development. Therefore, any economic system must recognize what is basic human motivation.

There seems nothing intrinsically wrong therefore, in an economic system that takes into account that human beings have as part of their nature an inherent eye on some personal advantage and minimum safety for themselves and their families. This is true even when one reckons with the fact that, within certain limits, human nature can be remarkably changed by the power of the Holy Spirit.

All great movements of economic growth have relied on the ingenuity, the tenacity, the willingness to overcome all obstacles, and very often the sacrifice of individuals working in the first instance for their own advantage. From the Christian point of view, the one essential requirement of such a system, if it is based on what might at first sight be regarded as an ignoble concept, is that the personal advantage never involves the sacrifice of any other, or if it is a question of one business succeeding and another failing because the latter is not so strong or efficient or does not have so dynamic a leadership, then there must be some way of safeguarding those who suffer.

This, however, is less easy to ensure than it sounds, for if you are to put the person who has failed in as strong a position as a person who has succeeded you take away all incentive for anyone to succeed. One of our present problems, as we have seen, is the fact that Social Security Benefits in the interest of compassion, and indeed Christian conviction, have been raised to such an extent that many feel that it is scarcely worth while going out to work. When a nation reaches this stage some believe it is in danger of becoming effete.

The British way is one of compromise, and it does not seem to be entirely outside the realm of human ingenuity to build up a system which does allow the individual as much freedom as is necessary to give full weight to his inventive and self-oriented instincts, whilst at the same time ensuring that the society that is being built is humane, compassionate and conscious at all time that no one is ultimately a sufferer. Many might well criticize such a philosophy on the grounds that it is tinkering with a system that is collapsing and that Christians must opt for a nobler theory. The difficulty about this sentiment is that such a theory, if it exists, is likely to prove far nobler in concept than execution. Far better is a system known for its weaknesses, that is capable of improvement, than one that promises heaven but in practice delivers a fair imitation of hell.

Some might argue that ultimately it does not matter in what sort of an economic system a Christian lives. All produce pain and a balance of advantage or disadvantage, and it is part of the overall learning through the harshness of early conditions that enables a Christian to develop in the presence of God his own spiritual life and character. Whilst this may be true, there seems no reason why we should suffer under a system which is harsher than it need be, and for that reason the best Christian and economic minds need to be deployed to develop one that can still prove to be as beneficial materially to humanity as possible.

There are, however, serious problems for the Christian in the modern social order, no matter what economic system is chosen. With each there is the developing problem of man against machine. As employers found that more and more work could be completed quicker and cheaper by utilizing modern machinery, so a greater number of employees were laid off. From the days of the Luddites workers have naturally been suspicious of new machinery. Generally unions are today more enlightened, providing there are advantages to their members, although naturally they often strike a hard bargain. Dockers, for example, have accepted containerization only after a bitter struggle which won for them substantial concessions.

Two issues of this type have a particular and almost insoluble moral conundrum. One relates to the difficulties facing factories situated in poor countries owned by companies in wealthy nations. Moral indignation might well result in considerable pressure being exerted to ensure that much higher wages are paid. Often the company replies that the fact of competitive life is such that either they continue to employ large numbers at comparatively low wages, or they employ many fewer and teach them how to use machines of the sort that are at present utilized in the West.

The other problem is similar but right inside our front door. Those who have done any real thinking about the future of solid-state technology and the integrated electronic circuits that are produced, are certain that (a) the circuits will be produced exceptionally cheaply and yet infinitely more complex than they are now; (b) they will have such a vastly increased range of application than at present; (c) there will scarcely be a trade or profession that is not very seriously affected. Alarmist projections indicate that possibly up to 5 million people in this country could be out of work in ten years' time. Even the most skilled human endeavour is in danger of being emulated by sophisticated machinery. The knowledge achieved by hospital consultants over a lifetime's work, for example, could be committed to a computer which would be directly accessible to an ordinary G.P. The movement of all forms of transport could be electronically controlled; cars could be produced with no human hands being involved except in servicing the machinery of construction.

So great are the dangers and yet so wonderful the prospects that Christians today should be considering with the greatest urgency whether (a) we should opt in to this technical revolution and provide an alternative human activity to work, or (b) opt out and let other nations take the wealth and decide to continue with our present machinery. (India, for example, in some instances deliberately refuses to mass produce so that she can give employment to the greatest numbers.)

In the end it is doubtful whether one can sustain an ostrich-like policy to modern technology. Huge changes therefore are necessary in our approach to work and leisure.

'City speculators', like 'gnomes of Zurich', has become a perjorative term for those who are against the market economy. It must be admitted that there are some both in the City of London and in the international money markets, who operate in anti-social ways, buying stock they do not intend to keep and selling stock they do not possess. The activities of the few cannot be taken to represent the attitudes of the many. Like any other institution, the stock market and international money markets have their share of black sheep.

Joint stock companies grew apace in the wake of the Industrial Revolution. They were formed because they represented the best way of gathering sufficient capital to finance wealth-producing operations. Individuals who had expertise but insufficient capital joined with others who had money only, for the mutual benefit of both.

Gradually a sophisticated system emerged whereby, particularly in the larger companies, shares could be sold by those wanting to realize their assets to those wanting to invest money. Stock exchanges were formed in different parts of the country, but from the beginning the one in London became the most important, setting what eventually became national prices for shares on a daily basis.

Many who are unfamiliar with the Stock Exchange tend to think of it as equivalent to a gambling casino. Essentially, however, it is like any other market—a place where items are bought and sold. Most people, when they have something to sell, seek the best price for it and when purchasing want to buy as cheaply as they can.

With many articles, there are times to buy and times to sell. People do not seek to sell a house or a car in the week before Christmas, for example, whereas in the spring when people are more tempted to purchase, a seller is more likely to be successful. When demand is lower, there is a tendency for prices to be less, too.

Such demand and supply cycles can be found in many markets, but on the Stock Exchange they are very much more pronounced, more frequent and certainly much more complicated.

All kinds of factors affect the prices of shares, and all contribute to a surplus of demand or supply. Performance of individual companies is, of course, important, as is an assessment of the quality of their management and future prospects. Certain external factors such as the Budget or the discovery of new processes or materials can have a big impact on a whole sector or sectors.

Unfortunately the Stock Market is hyper-sensitive to the smallest snippet of information and often reacts much more strongly than the news deserves. This is especially true of economic information. A favourable report from an influential body can cause the market to open up and trigger off a round of buying. On the other hand, unexpectedly poor results from a major company or some unfavourable economic indicator can similarly start a bout of selling.

A further complication lies in the fact that the market tends to *anticipate* events rather than react to them. Thus, a view is formed, for example of what the next monthly Trade figures will be like, and shares will move up or down prior to the announcement. Reaction after publication is usually only in respect of how far the figures lived up to expectation.

Various movements can take place for technical reasons—e.g. a technical rally caused by buying at a time when there is a shortage of stock.

The Stock Market is therefore one of the most sophisticated markets in the world, and perhaps for that reason, the most open to misunderstanding. None the less, in so far as it puts buyers in touch with sellers, and facilitates the formation of new capital to be used in wealth-producing exercises, it performs a most useful social function.

The only alternative to this kind of activity is a State-planned economy. This brings us again to the realm of the politics of money.

Theologically, socially and morally, the Christian is committed to wealth-producing, and to using the assets of the community to wrest from the earth its fruits in ways that are most beneficial to mankind. The major problem is one of distribution, but that is not the concern of investment.

13 Church investment

To many the position of these two words might appear incongruous. However, having earlier acknowledged that it is right for the Church to own property and having assured oneself that the Church has conducted its affairs in the most efficient and sensitive way possible, and having accepted that the Church must plan to meet its responsibilities in the future, it is left with the problem of how to deal with the sums of money that are available.

A local church can, of course, manage its small sums of money by using a Building Society or some other low-yield investment, but it is clear that greatly improved arrangements can be made if investment is managed centrally. Large sums of money can then be operated and a very sophisticated system of facilities can be made available that cater for every conceivable requirement, from money available for only a few days, to money that will not be required for twenty or thirty years. As soon as one reaches this point, one is involved in big money, for with up to ten thousand churches, many of which have some money available for future use, millions of pounds is soon amassed centrally. Originally, under the old Trust Acts, churches had an overwhelming porportion of their assets in Fixed Interest Securities, these being considered the only safe investment available. However, the last decades have shown that Fixed Interest Securities can be a danger, especially the undated ones; War Loan, for example. Many who purchased this stock at over 100 can remember painfully that it has been quoted with a market value as low as 18.

For those responsible for investments only thirty years ago, life was comparatively simple in that the only thing needed was a degree of financial skill. Things are very different today, however, for not only is the financial expertise required very much greater, with the movement of Church funds into equity shares, but all kinds of ramifications arise when the ethical implications of equity investments are considered.

The movement into equity investments (the purchase of shares in public companies) took place in the late fifties and early sixties and there are two main reasons. Firstly, it was considered in those days one of the best ways to combat inflation, the underlying philosophy being that owners of equities had a share in the tangible assets of a company and no matter how the value of currency was eroded, the underlying assets would maintain their real value. This may still be true in the very long term—over a period of decades—but in the past few years we have seen the value of the currency depreciating rapidly though the value of shares has not increased.

Other pressures, such as Government restrictions of dividends, lack of confidence in the whole economic system, and lack of competitive edge, have caused shares to lose their real value rather than to rise. Providing money is not required on a very short-term basis and one can choose one's time to realise assets, the equity market might still be right financially for much Church investment.

Another reason, however, for the Church going into equities was that it was considered to be a way of sharing in the production of new wealth. In the past few years, one of the things that has held the economy of this country back has been the lack of new investment. Taxation, confidence and other reasons are given for this and it could well be argued that the Church has a responsibility to ensure that the money that it has amassed for future use should be deployed in a way that will add to the general wealth of the community rather than being determined by narrow financial interest. Money held on behalf of others, however, can never be recklessly deployed even in pursuit of laudable aims, though the investor often does have some degree of flexibility in his choice of investments.

The Church has always felt it important to ensure that its purchase of shares in no way compromised the moral standards that it has sought to uphold in its teaching and it was thought entirely inappropriate that it should possess shares in any company that produced goods or services which could be construed as being against those standards. For example, the Methodist Church would not purchase the shares of companies involved in the production of armaments. Neither would it be willing to become involved with companies producing alcoholic drink or tobacco, or which were involved with gambling. For a number of years this selective approach to investment was considered the only way that the Church could exercise its responsibilities.

In more recent years, however, this has been felt inadequate, for two reasons. First, it was felt that the Church should be more involved in the day-to-day running of the companies in which it was a shareholder; second, with the enormous upsurge of takeovers, particularly in the 1960s, companies had interests which covered a multitude of things, some of which might be considered to be unacceptable. The desire for 'clean money' is virtually incapable of being fulfilled in this imperfect world, if the point is pressed far enough. For example, the Methodist Church has never invested in breweries and it would not invest in wine merchants, but because of takeovers and diversifications some very well-known companies, such as Marks and Spencer and other supermarket chains, sometimes sell wines. If one were to cut out all companies with even a subsidiary interest in this particular field, one would soon have nothing left to invest in except Building Societies, Government fixed-interest stocks, or Local Authorities. It is not unknown, however, for local authorities to own public houses, nor for governments to spend their money in ways that from time to time Christians feel thoroughly undesirable. Even Building Societies have to invest a certain proportion of their funds to protect their liquidity, and it might well be that the most innocent looking Building Society account contains a fractional percentage of an interest in, say, a supermarket store that is involved in selling alcohol.

The Church still resolutely refuses to invest in companies that are wholly or mainly engaged in things that it considers undesirable, but we recognize that it is impossible to be completely free from any investment whatsoever. Another reason for a change in policy is that the Churches have considered it important, not merely to have a passive approach to ethical investment, but also to have a positive one, and this involves recognizing that as a shareholder one becomes a part-owner of the company and therefore shares in the moral responsibility for its activities.

Experience over recent years has shown that, contrary to general opinion, Company Chairmen and Directors are interested in the views of their shareholders and do take note of points that are raised. There are two ways in which issues can be raised in a company. For a substantial shareholder—and many Church investing bodies approach or already merit this description—often the most effective method is to write a letter or to see the Chairman of the Company and discuss the particular issue in confidence, knowing that it can be dealt with in another way if eventually this proves ineffective. Many Company Chairmen go to considerable lengths to ensure that their shareholders are kept fully informed once they raise a particular issue. The other method, of course, is to deal with the matter publicly, either by selling shares with an accompanying Press statement, or alternatively tabling a Resolution at an Annual General Meeting. This latter method was used in the case of the Midland Bank's loans to South Africa. Considerable discussion with the Company beforehand had not produced any real effect and in two successive years resolutions were tabled requiring the Directors not to make loans to the South African Government or its agencies. Indeed, the first one, tabled in the name of the Central

Church investment

Finance Board of the Methodist Church, was believed to be the first resolution on a moral issue that had ever been put before an Annual General Meeting in this country. That exercise was organized by a small group of enthusiastic anti-apartheid campaigners. It resulted in considerable success in that although the institutional block votes inevitably won the decision for the directors, in the end they conceded the main point and ceased lending money direct to the South African Government. In two years this particular policy, aided by other companies abroad, and worsening conditions in South Africa which made loans less attractive commercially, was sufficient to ensure a change of direction of most of the major banks in this country.

To raise a particular issue at a company meeting involves interested shareholders in a great amount of work. First of all, one hundred shareholders have to agree to the form of wording and the Law requires that substantial capital has to be held, to avoid a hundred people with only one share each taking resolutions. Fortunately or unfortunately, the Churches do not have the capacity, either financially or in manpower terms, to mount such resolutions very frequently and therefore it is necessary to utilize shareholder pressure more subtly although possibly just as effectively. Directors can often be given firm indications of shareholders' views which will enable them to shift direction easily, whereas very frequently in a company Annual General Meeting when facing criticism they feel they have their backs to the wall and cannot shift; in these circumstances the major institutional shareholders almost invariably support the Directors, unless there is great financial dissatisfaction over their policies.

Quite a lot has been done by Church shareholders, particularly on the South African issues. Controversy has ranged within the Churches on the objects to be attained by such pressure, one view being that the Churches should utilize their holdings to ensure a responsible approach by

113

companies seeking to improve the lot of coloured workers. Others have felt that complete withdrawal should be forced upon companies so that their activities in South Africa should be abandoned, thus isolating the country completely. At a theoretical level this particular discussion goes on and perhaps will go on until apartheid is abandoned. However, those charged with the responsibility of investment find it very difficult to understand how a company could conceivably withdraw from South Africa without incurring unreasonable financial loss which the Directors would not contemplate nor would they be permitted to cease business voluntarily, under company law. They would not be allowed to throw away assets for a political motive. The sale of such assets would not be likely to do the coloured people of South Africa any material good, as they would be purchased by other companies, perhaps with a less responsible ethical attitude. If at any point such withdrawal policies look like doing any injury to the South African Government, they would be able quickly to enact legislation prohibiting such moves. The only effective action that appears remotely possible is through government legislation, preferably with international agreement.

Thus it is, that those with investment responsibility within the Churches have sought to use the alternative strategy of pressing companies on all kinds of matters, in the hope of improving conditions for the black and coloured workers of South Africa. Amongst the objectives sought after are an improvement in wages, better working conditions and opportunities, medical and training facilities and even legal advice.

Following a newspaper article by Mr Adam Raphael in the *Guardian* in 1973 and the consequent pressure brought by the Churches and others on companies, the wages of black South Africans rose quite dramatically, but even this could not be regarded as an unmitigated success for two reasons. One was that unemployment also increased as companies found it better to use machines rather than human labour, because the latter had become too expensive; second, other social problems arose as particularly black workers, given greatly increased wages without adequate training and help on how to use their increased wealth, tended to squander much of it, and the incidence of drunkenness and alcoholism have risen dramatically.

None the less, it is certain that pressure towards equal pay is being successful, and as the level of consumer spending of black and coloured workers increases, so does their consumer power. It also appears more and more nonsensical to have the petty apartheid restrictions that have existed. One by one these are disappearing, but at the time of writing there is little sign of any real dent in the basic injustices of the system, whereby the black and coloured people of that land, although in a vast majority, have no say in the political affairs of the country nor any real share in its wealth.

Since shareholders have become interested in ethical considerations, not only have operations in South Africa been subjected to scrutiny, but many other activities throughout the world have also been investigated. Drug companies have been pressed regarding their politics, particularly in under-developed countries. Questions have been raised regarding unhealthy conditions, environmental issues and labour relations.

What acts as the biggest block in increasing pressure all round, is the time and research that is necessary before one is in a position legitimately and helpfully to criticize the policy of a company. It is hoped that as the years go by and more Churches and others seek to follow this line of activity, increasingly people will become aware of the issues involved and will themselves ensure that these particular problems are faced fully. It is not suggested that companies would always be unethical in their approach were it not for the pressure brought by certain shareholders. Indeed, there is every evidence that many management decisions are taken on the basis of a very high level of ethical responsibility, although there are a number of important exceptions. The alertness of a free and occasionally hypocritical Press which often takes a delight in dramatic and sometimes lurid revelations, and makes the most of ethical deviations, none the less has the effect of a useful public watch dog. This sometimes stimulates legislation which reduces the unethical behaviour which can be indulged in without penalty. Today's sailing near the wind is often tomorrow's crime.

One of the problems about this particular trend is that in a sense the City tends to become more and more bound by a legal tangle which could reduce profitable activity much in the same way that religion was entangled by the pharisaical approach to the Law. The release of the Christian spirit within any economic system must be of ultimate advantage to the community as a whole in that it helps people to do the right things for the right reasons rather than to be chivied unwillingly along certain legally defined lines. The trend away from unethical practices which operate to the detriment of the community as a whole has been accelerating, but attention has always been paid to capital and the capitalist, mainly for the obvious reason that from the earliest days the greatest danger to society came from the unethical entrepreneur, who was not particular as to how he made his money so long as profit could be achieved.

It is interesting, however, that now that the unions have properly achieved a sense of power and are well able to safeguard the interests of their members, there are considerable dangers of unethical practices being perpetrated by unions or by members of unions. Writers frequently compare the power of British unions with their counterparts in other strong capitalist societies such as the U.S.A. or Western Germany, illustrating this with graphic details of over-manning being forced on employers (like the printing industry), railway workers requiring over-manning on railway train cabs, insisting on two people travelling (when one is all that is necessary), and workers insisting on all kinds of safeguards for their particular members which act against the public good.

How these unethical practices are to be dealt with remains a problem that the Church and others as well as the industries concerned must come to grips with. It is not easy to see how this can be achieved. The traditional sights of the Churches' ethical artillery has always been lined up against the employers and it does not come easy to sweep those sights round to a different target, particularly as this could very quickly be regarded as 'anti-union'. However, if the Church is interested in truth it cannot be muzzled merely because certain things it must say render it liable to misrepresentation. If a man is put out of work despite his conscientious objections, through the 'closed shop' issue, or by forcing a company into an uncompetitive position, the Church must say that the situation is immoral and that anti-social behaviour is being shown by unions. If it can be proved to exist, it must be opposed just as fiercely as anti-social behaviour by employers: for example, those employers who are implacably opposed to any form of union activity at all. In the autumn of 1977 there were signs that the Church and community were becoming increasingly angered at the way in which a succession of workers went on strike, either officially or unofficially, to achieve a breakdown of the Government's pay policy. Canon Collins, a noted left-winger, voiced these feelings in St Paul's Cathedral on Sunday, 6th November, and described the power-workers' unofficial strike as 'an outrage against human life . . . . It is the public that is being taken hostage, and it is the weakest, those who are most unable to fend for themselves, the old, the sick, who are made to suffer.'

These matters of industrial relations, however, are not easily improved by those outside the scene. It would be much better for the opposition to unethical behaviour relating to unions to come from within, from Christians who are union members, and it is only when the clamour of opposition to certain actions becomes strong enough that the State and the legislators are able to take over and outlaw unacceptable excesses from whatever source.

The most important aim of all is the development of a personal sensitivity to Christian ideals in all areas, whether at management, union or investment level. The idealist performs a useful function in pointing the way to what should be achieved if it were possible. Unfortunately, idealists often strain credulity to the point of despair. Those who write and speak idealistically also have an ethical responsibility towards those who are operating, not in a vacuum, but in the hard, sometimes sharp, shingle of reality.

14 Money and relationships

Earlier, when examining the profit motive, we discussed the fact that the instinct of self-interest was deeply ingrained in human nature and had been so since the beginning, when man emerged triumphant over the animal kingdom. It still plays a big part in human behaviour, and it is worth while to pursue the instinctive motivation of man a little further, because it deeply affects not only his behaviour and relationship with others, but through these his attitude to money. *Homo sapiens* has always been prepared to defend itself when attacked, and this had been the secret of its survival, as it is in the case of the majority of the animal world. The more subtle the creature that develops, the more complicated his defensive mechanisms. The animal kingdom has many instances of the 'own territory' syndrome, the willingness, indeed the compulsion, to defend what one considers one's own area. Any intruder is swiftly attacked for daring to act as interloper on ground that has been annexed.

In the animal kingdom the defender has to remain awake and remain in occupation twenty-four hours a day for fear someone else takes over. Many animal and bird lovers marvel at the way in which an intense alertness is kept up for so long. Human beings have learned to use locks and keys, banks and other methods of securing wealth, such as burglar alarms and the employment of private security firms. Most significant of all is the development of a police force entrusted with the keeping of law and order with great emphasis on property rights.

Despite the development of security measures and devices, however, in caring for one's property it is easy for things to get out of balance. As we saw, Jesus himself recognized this when he warned against the dangers of a wealth which requires too much of one's resources to care for or safeguard. There are, however, many developments of this peculiarity which human beings can evince. Some people are much too sensitive of their own 'rights' with regard to the intrusion of other people's noise, or extend the boundaries of their house to the road outside and object to others parking in 'their space'.

These traits appear sometimes at their most severe when what are regarded as attacks on one's own wealth are mounted. For example, one of the greatest causes of unhappiness between next-door neighbours is often a fence that is required to be repaired or a tree whose roots are alleged to have damaged the foundations of a neighbour's house. One of the developments towards a true Christian maturity must surely be that these defensive mechanisms are recognized and kept very carefully in check. For example, a Christian ought to find it very difficult to develop a concept of absolute ownership. He recognizes that God himself is the true owner and he is merely a steward. Whilst a good steward is very careful about his master's property, he is less likely to develop a neurosis or an exaggerated view of what is owned, particularly as he recognizes that other people are also stewards of the same master, and if life is to proceed with a minimum of disruption and not to become intolerable, there must be a continual measure of accommodation with others.

In some personalities these basically defensive mechanisms become more offensive through a pre-emptive strike to gain power over others. Sometimes the urge for power is unconscious in that the person involved becomes engrossed in a particular enterprise and only indirectly or perhaps subconsciously does he assume a position of power, and sometimes great power, over others. Power derives partly from position, but position itself is usually associated with the money base of the person concerned. It may not even be his own money but if he is in control of a large company, or even a small one, he has power over many.

The reasons why people like power are numerous. One is that hidden in the psychological recesses of their mind, most people want to be liked. They want to be well thought of and even looked up to. In many instances, although not all, a man is looked up to for his prowess, which usually has some financial reward which in turn strengthens his position. Although perhaps they would not admit it, people are impressed by wealth in others and accede to them positions of authority that are not always deserved. Another reason (or perhaps a development of the previous one) is that some people gain great satisfaction in providing or withholding something at whim. An elementary example of this phenomenon is the way in which even many adults like feeding the birds in the park. It may be that they do it to study and enjoy bird behaviour, but a more devious psychological explanation might suggest that they find a subconscious pleasure in a sense of power over another living thing. Such a power is exercised over an uncomplicated subject. It requires a more forceful and complicated personality to take pleasure in a real power over people; this may develop unacceptably into 'manipulation'. Thus are sown the seeds of even a micro-dictator.

The more wealth or power a person achieves, the more his personality develops an attitude which assumes power and money as of right without question. Here begins the well-known process of corruption which is attributable to power. A Christian view of wealth breaks through the Gordian knot of ever-increasing complication and allows a Christian, if he has wealth or power, to sit lightly upon it, to accept it while it is his, to accept its removal if that is to be; he is released from the intensity of trying to keep what he can, and thus from the absolute corruption that ultimately awaits him.

Another curious instinct is that of the collector, known even in Biblical times. It is quite closely related to the instinct for power, but is rather more passive. It seeks to acquire a greater and greater amount of whatever is collected, whatever it be: stamps, coins, matchboxes, or horse brasses. In many instances it engenders a desire for completeness, and develops a dissatisfaction if either a better specimen is discovered or an incomplete set is in his possession. Very often such hobbies are quite harmless and indeed add considerably to one's knowledge of human behaviour and geography. Once again, however, the degree of involvement of the human personality with the 'wealth' of the collection, its improvement or advancement, determines whether or not the exercise is one that is justifiable in Christian terms and beneficial to human personality and relationships. Too great a commitment or involvement means that the individual's values become unbalanced, and his sense of proportion distorted. In the worse case he can become so neurotically attached that his relationships with others are damaged, for he sees them as potential enemies in his search for improvement.

One motive that often promotes a desire for wealth is one which derives from the instinct of protection of one's own young. With most human parents there is a desire to ensure that one's young are well treated and have as good an opportunity as possible to develop and share in the wealth of the country. With some, however, imbalance is achieved and a neurotic compulsion develops to seek more than normal support for children. This sometimes is demonstrated by the dedication of too high a proportion of normal income to the education of children, sometimes a passionate desire to produce sufficient wealth oneself to ensure that they have all the good things that are available. Occasionally it triggers off an overwhelming need to achieve riches so that one's children can be protected from all possible contingencies deriving from lack of money.

Such desires are often very bad in terms of relationships in that what is done often affects the children of friends or neighbours. Often the advancement of one's young can only be achieved at the expense of the children of others, in terms of educational facilities which are of limited availability. Alternatively, the building up of one's own children is reached by denigrating those who have *not* achieved such benefits. The human personality becomes almost reincarnated in the personalities of one's children and a sense of proportion is then lost and is not regained until suddenly the children reach the age when they leave home. If the attitude is continued beyond adolescence it is at the expense of the developing personality of the children themselves. More often than not, however, the child itself reacts rather violently to parental 'over-protection' and throws it off in a manner that creates utter surprise and maximum unhappiness in the foolish parent.

Some individuals find it very difficult to live normally without extra excitement and risk. This taste for primeval adrenalin-producing activity is sometimes found in the criminal who will take all kinds of risks in order to gain greater wealth. Often the gain is considered not to be at the expense of others because mistakenly it is thought that a bank, an insurance company or a jeweller can well afford to lose what is stolen.

Risk taking can also lead to all kinds of gambling. Occasionally, if it is taken to an ultimate extreme, whole families break up because of the intensity of the desire and the impossibility of breaking from it. For many human beings the desire for excitement is satisfied without recourse to wealth considerations: for example, at a football match or some other sporting activity; but for others this has an air of unreality and does not produce the additional benefits that are thought to be derived from attaching the risk-taking to a wealth-producing activity.

The primitive human emotion of envy, disliked and disapproved of for centuries, can be contained within the mind or sublimated in some other way, but when it becomes related to wealth it can produce all kinds of human problems and difficult relationships. A typical instance is the way in which relatives, normally on good terms with each other, can suddenly become very worked up about a Will. Because of a desire to achieve through the vehicle of a deceased's Estate the maximum benefit, many such quarrels have lasted a lifetime and have been totally disastrous both in terms of relationships and of the development of the human personality concerned.

Smouldering envy of the wealth or achievements of others has sometimes developed into a hatred that destroys friendship. Envy secretly fermenting can also ruin the peace of mind of an individual who dwells on what is considered to be utterly unfair, making the dubious assumption that all are entitled to the same wealth. A relaxed Christian attitude to the possessions of others can be interpreted as a supine acknowledgment of injustice, but to those who have gained the spiritual pearl of great price, the fact that someone else has a shiny piece of quartz is of supreme irrelevance.

Of course, negative and undesirable applications of instincts are not the only ones that can be seen. There are many positive examples of human activity which when translated into wealth terms indicate the best achievements of human nature. For example, compassion. The sudden desire to do something for one less fortunate than oneself must go back into the mists of human envolvement. Compassion and generosity need to be exercised with some judicial care, for in terms of relationships they can generate feelings of envy and dissatisfaction in others. Compassion lavished on one individual only, when he is one among many others, could quite easily produce, not just satisfaction in the individual concerned, but much dissatisfaction amongst all the others around. A net result inferior to the situation before the act of compassion took place could easily ensue. Many tourists in poor countries have learnt the danger of feeling sorry for an isolated little child who happens to beg for money. When such child receives a few coins, in a very short time scores more children appear, all clamouring for the same treatment. When more cash is not forthcoming, there is widespread dissatisfaction among them.

A very large proportion of people act in conformity with the established practices of society. An instinctive desire to please, to satisfy and indeed to draw as little attention as possible to self, produces a group of conformists, without which society is unable to operate. The community only proceeds with a degree of smoothness if the very large majority are prepared to accept a single, broad set of rules. Such is the perversity of human nature that one often tends to praise a nonconformist because he exhibits a degree of individualism and tenacity of purpose that represents personality of a high calibre. Very often it is the nonconformists and those who object to the norm that keep society moving or progressing but the great problem is to decide which elements of nonconformity are acceptable and which are not. The criterion is not necessarily whether in the immediate future the attitude appears to hurt society. Those who saw financial ruin staring them in the face on the abolition of slavery must have felt that the nonconformists who were changing the opinion of society were gravely injuring the future prospects of the nation. They have, however, in the event been proved to be wrong.

On the other extreme, nonconformists that rob, either individual members of the community or institutions like banks, have over the centuries been regarded as anti-social and thoroughly undesirable. Somewhat in the middle, perhaps, are those nonconformists whose actions have yet to be proved either desirable or undesirable: for example, some workers' co-operatives emanating from 'sit-ins', where production continues after a company has decided it wishes to cease trading. Even Unions appear unsettled and equivocal in their judgements regarding this unusual behaviour. What is increasingly clear in the financial scene as well as in society generally is that a community can only accept a very limited number of nonconformists, otherwise the whole system breaks down. Society owes more than is generally acknowledged to the vast bulk of the population who dislike appearing different from others, either in the realm of norms of dress or behaviour or financial attitudes.

Conformity in the financial as well as the social sense could be regarded as a form of inertia or laziness, but more often than not it is to be judged a type of caring—a sensitivity to the rights, privileges, and susceptibilities of others in society.

The more one examines the motives which trigger certain financial attitudes and behaviour, the more one comes eventually to the conclusion that, as was assumed in the first chapter, money does not have a life of its own, but all money movement is determined by human behaviour and attitudes.

It follows, therefore, that there is no hope for a kind of financial Utopia unless men behave in a thoroughly altruistic fashion, after the manner of Jesus. Actions can only be regarded as good in so far as they accord with the will of God, in so far as that can be ascertained. This latter can normally be regarded as another facet of behaviour which can be regarded as beneficial for society, either in the obvious short-run or in the not-so-obvious, long-term results.

Good behaviour, however, does not emanate from the bad man except by accident, in which case it has no moral value nor any long term contribution to the benefit of society. The fact that the financial scene is morally very patchy is only a reflection of a society that accepts both moral rectitude and immoral aberration, both in the individual and in society as a whole. A financial Utopia involves the development of sustained goodness in people, or, to express it theoretically, in a spiritual movement towards the Kingdom of God.

It is not altogether easy to visualize the Kingdom of Heaven translated into material terms. One example, however, can be given. Those who served in the Forces during the war knew what it was like to live in a society where, although occasionally there was compassion and heroic bravery, the norm was 'everyone for himself', and this could be discovered in many attitudes where 'number one' was the being served. Apart from isolated relationships of friendship, one could never be sure how others would behave, and a tube of toothpaste left in the wash room would be certain to have vanished in a few minutes and any item of real value much quicker than that. The transformation, however, when such an individual went to live in some Christian community where all had dedicated themselves to Jesus Christ, was quite remarkable, for the principle dominating every part of behaviour was the love of others as demonstrated by God in Jesus. Although perfection was not to be expected, it was very rare to find other than genuine care and compassion in every relationship and the tube of toothpaste and even much more valuable things could be found where they had been left or, alternatively, in the appropriate lost property department.

In so far as the enactments of the State are way behind the norms acceptable for genuine Christian behaviour, Christians must always strive for an advancing front in the direction of morality. This is one important contribution Christians make towards the implementation of a more just society. Genuine financial morality, however, must spring from individuals dedicated to God, transformed by God and alert at all times to the prompting of God, though this of course is not to assert that goodness is the monopoly of Christians.

Today, as never before, Christians must demonstrate that their faith is not a theoretical exercise to be performed by a few religiously inclined cranks; it is a relevant and dynamic factor in everyday practical living. Obviously it is feasible, and indeed frequently demonstrated, that man can operate in this world without any regard for God. As a comparatively free individual he can opt to please himself and operate as selfishly, destructively and as immorally as the law allows. His attitude to money and financially related actions can be as ruthless as the community permits.

The Christian has seen a better way, and one that is demonstrably better for society. As each choice presents itself he relates it to Christ's teaching; as each decision has to be made he seeks to know the will of God; in dreaming of the future his telescope is abandoned in favour of a clear unaided sight of the attainable, even if, unnoticed there are stars in the unachievable distance twinkling from the same compass point. He is a man under authority, and his wealth and possessions are ultimately not his to command. He acts as an efficient manager on a comparatively short business trip dealing with assets for which he is responsible and in accordance with Company policy. His tenure of office in comparison with the life of the Company is short, just as the Christian's spell of 70 years or so on earth is short compared with eternity.

The Christian's pleasure is found in relating the material things under his control to the purposes of God. Whilst he has them, he enjoys them; if they are taken away he will ruefully miss them, but find some other way of expressing his thanks to God.

Having been given the raw material of his own personality, under God's guidance as a craftsman he seeks to shape it under the sharp tools of life's experiences. Flaws are sometimes revealed, but use can be made of them in the execution of the ultimate design. Mistakes are made in the shaping—sometimes they can be eradicated—but occasionally they have to be left to the forgiving eye of the Beholder—stark, even ugly, but wholly human.

Money becomes a way in which the personality expresses itself: it is both a means of projection and a method of judgement. It is a God-given gift but not one to be treated casually; it can enhance, it can destroy. Used as intended it is not only the coinage of the realm, it becomes the currency of the Kingdom.